OCEANS

An Activity Guide for Ages 6–9

Nancy F. Castaldo

CHICAGO
REVIEW
PRESS

Library of Congress Cataloging-in-Publication Data

Castaldo, Nancy F. (Nancy Fusco), 1962–

    Oceans : an activity guide for ages 6–9 / Nancy F. Castaldo.

        p. cm.

    Includes bibliographical references and index.

    ISBN 1-55652-443-9

    1. Oceanography—Study and teaching (Elementary)—
Activity programs.

GC31.35 .C37 2002

372.3'5—dc21

Cover and interior design: Monica Baziuk
Cover and interior illustration: B. Kulak

First edition
Published by Chicago Review Press, Incorporated
814 North Franklin Street
Chicago, Illinois 60610
ISBN 1-55652-443-9
Printed in the United States of America
5 4 3 2 1

"To stand at the edge of the sea, to sense the ebb and the flow of the tides,

to feel the breadth of a mist moving over a great salt marsh, to watch the flight of shorebirds

that have swept up and down the surf lines of the continents for untold thousands of years,

to see the running of the old eels and the young shad to the sea,

is to have the knowledge of things that are as nearly eternal as any earthly life can be."

—RACHEL CARSON, naturalist and author of *The Silent Spring*

For my parents and the rest of my family who haven't been

able to shake the sand from their toes.

Contents

Acknowledgments

Many thanks to Dr. Thierry Chopin, professor of marine biology, University of New Brunswick, Centre for Coastal Studies and Aquaculture; Peter Haddow, director, Seal Conservation Society, and Ellen Pikitch, of the Wildlife Conservation Society's marine program, for their expertise in answering my many questions; and Lynn Minderman, curriculum and instructional specialist, Chatham Central School District, for her valuable insight. A special thanks also to Lisa Rosenthal and Cynthia Sherry, who make work fun.

Introduction

"Beyond all things is the ocean."

—SENECA

The Roman philosopher Seneca wrote these words close to two thousand years ago. It's still true, isn't it? If you decided to walk continuously in one direction from wherever you were, you would eventually come to an ocean. It may not be on the same day that you started your walk or in the same week or even month, but eventually you would reach the shore.

Once upon a time people did not believe the world was round. In fact, many thought that the world ended in the ocean off the coast of Spain. We know now that the ocean doesn't end. It wraps around the whole world, and the future of our planet depends upon it. That's why we need to study the ocean and protect it.

Oceans is written for everyone who is inspired by the ocean, whether or not you have ever dipped your feet in its waters. Alone and in groups, kids will enjoy activities that explore the world beneath the waves. They'll find out about their favorite ocean creatures and what they can do to help them. Facts will pop out in *"Ocean Notion"* sidebars, and ideas for more fun appear under the heading *"Ocean Challenges"* at the end of the book. Most of all, kids will discover a new frontier that they'll want to explore again and again. So turn the page and start getting wild about oceans!

Catch a Wave

Imagine you are flying in a spaceship above the planet Earth. What do you think the earth looks like from outer space? It looks blue! That's because the earth's oceans and seas cover about three quarters of the earth's surface. Now imagine you are standing on a beach along the East Coast of the United States. Waves splash up to the shore and touch your toes. It may be hard to imagine, but those waves splashing up on the beach may have traveled thousands of miles to reach you. In fact, some of that ocean water may have touched a toe in Hawaii or splashed up against a sailboat off the coast of Australia. Some of that water may have even traveled past the coast of Japan or melted from a glacier floating in the Arctic Ocean.

It is possible for ocean water to travel from ocean to ocean because the earth's five oceans—the Atlantic, Pacific, Arctic, Indian, and Antarctic—are all connected, making them actually one huge body of water. Take a look at a globe. Can you move your finger to each ocean without lifting it or touching any landmasses?

Read a Tide Chart

If you stand in one spot near the edge of the ocean for a while, you will see that the water does not come up to the same spot in the sand every time a wave breaks. For part of the day, the water moves closer to where you are standing. Then for the rest of the day, it moves away from where you are standing. It is also easy to see this action on a wharf. For part of the day, the water is higher on the wharf. During the other part of the day, the water may be so low that it doesn't even reach the wharf. This action, called the *tide*, is caused by the power of the sun and moon. Gravity pulls on the water directly below the moon. This pull causes the ocean to bulge out toward the moon. As the earth rotates around the sun, different parts of the ocean directly face the moon, which keeps the tides changing. That is why the tide is not high nor low at the same time every day.

Twice a month the sun, moon, and Earth line up. When this happens, the sun and moon both pull on the water and the tide becomes higher and lower than usual.

It's best to look for shells on the beach during a low tide. Take a look at the tide chart on this page. What is the best time to look for shells on Wednesday? If you eat dinner at 5:30 P.M. on Saturday, would you plan to go to the beach before or after dinner?

Date	Time of High Tide	Time of Low Tide
Wednesday	11:54 P.M.	5:36 P.M.
Thursday	12:28 A.M.	5:44 P.M.
Friday	1:14 A.M.	6:51 P.M.
Saturday	12:58 P.M.	6:06 P.M.
Sunday	7:05 P.M.	12:31 A.M.
Monday	8:35 P.M.	1:43 A.M.
Tuesday	7:44 P.M.	12:57 A.M.

Toxic Red Tide

Named for their red-colored waves, *red tides* are tides that contain a higher-than-normal number of tiny ocean plants, or algae, known as *phytoplankton*, which is present in the ocean. This algae is poisonous to humans, fish, and other marine wildlife. Marine biologists are studying the algae and searching for ways to control future outbreaks. In order to control red tides, marine biologists must find answers to some important questions. Pretend you are a marine biologist. What questions do you think need answers?

What Is a Sea?

The Mediterranean, Baltic, Red, and Caribbean are bodies of water called seas. What's the difference between a sea and an ocean? Seas are smaller than oceans. A *sea* is usually a large body of salt water that is partially enclosed by land with a channel leading to an ocean. This definition is true of most seas, such as the Bering, Caribbean, Red, and Mediterranean seas. Some seas do not fit this definition and are not actually true seas. For example, the Sea of Galilee is a large body of freshwater. The Sargasso Sea and the Coral Sea are both found in a portion of an ocean and are not enclosed by any land. The Dead Sea is actually a saltwater lake because it is completely surrounded by land. The Dead Sea has so much salt that even saltwater fish cannot live in it.

How Does Salt Get into the Ocean?

Everyone knows that seawater is salty, but where does the salt come from? Why is it that some bodies of water are salty and others are not? Actually, all water has a bit of salt in it. It all starts with rainwater. The rain falls and seeps through the rocks and soil. As it does this, it dissolves some of the minerals, such as salt, and washes them into streams, lakes, and then into the ocean.

The amount of salt found in freshwater streams and lakes is so small that we cannot even taste it, but in the ocean the concentration of salt is far greater. Why is this so? Streams, lakes, and rivers have a constant flow of water in and out of them. Oceans, on the other hand, do not. The rivers bring water and salt into the ocean. The water evaporates into the air over time, but the salt remains in the seawater. The salt in the ocean has taken millions of years to accumulate to its present level. The Dead Sea contains salt for the same reason as the ocean: it has no outlet. The only flow of water out of the lake is through evaporation, so the salt stays in the lake.

Another source of ocean salt is underground volcanoes that erupt beneath the ocean surface. The seawater comes in contact with hot rock, dissolving some of its minerals into the ocean. Similarly, salt is also dissolved into the ocean through the hot water released by hydrothermal vents on the ocean floor. The hot water dissolves the minerals of the earth's crust at the bottom of the ocean floor. The difference in this process is that not only is salt released into the ocean, but some of the salt reacts with the basalt rock of the ocean crust and is removed from the water.

Scientists have found that the amount of salt in the ocean does not change, because new minerals are being created on the ocean floor at the same rate that salt is being removed from the water.

Why Is the Sea Salty? A Norwegian Tale

Many different cultures have created legends to explain the saltiness of seawater. Here is a tale from Norway. After reading it, see if you can make up your own tale to explain why the sea is salty.

Once upon a time there were two brothers, one rich and one poor. It came to pass that on Christmas Eve the poor brother came asking the rich one for something to eat. The rich brother was tired of hearing his brother ask for things, so before the poor brother had even reached the house, he called out to him, "If you will promise to do as I ask, I will give you one of the large hams that is hanging from the chimney."

The poor brother called back to him, "I promise."

With that the older brother threw down the ham and said, "Good. Now go away and never come begging here again."

The poor brother took his ham and walked away. On his way he met a man with a long, white beard.

"Good evening," said the old man. "Where are you headed?"

The poor brother stopped and nodded at the old man.

"I am going home to my wife."

"If you go just a bit farther you will come to an enchanter's castle. Go inside. You will be asked by the enchanter's trolls to sell your ham. Do not sell it, but instead trade it for an old coffee mill that rests beside the door you entered. Return to me with the coffee mill and I will tell you how to use it."

The poor brother thought it a bit strange but thanked the man and went on his way. After quite a while he finally reached the castle. He knocked on the huge door in front of him and instantly it opened. The trolls quickly surrounded him and asked for the ham, just as the old man had said. After much discussion, the trolls reluctantly agreed to trade the ham for the coffee mill.

The poor brother carried the coffee mill back to the place where he had met the old man. The old man had waited for his return and quickly showed the poor brother how to use the coffee mill. To set the mill in action he merely had to tell it what he wished for and turn the handle, but to make it stop he needed to turn it on its side. After thanking the kind old man, the poor brother turned toward his home. By the time he arrived, it was very late. His wife had waited for his return before beginning to prepare their holiday meal. When he arrived it was much too late to prepare anything. The poor brother placed the coffee mill on the table, wished for a splendid meal, and turned the handle of the mill. In an instant the table was covered with a beautiful tablecloth, candles, and enough food for a king! The two sat down and enjoyed the feast.

During the week after Christmas, the man and his wife gave a grand party for all of their friends and family. They used the coffee mill to provide food and drink for the party. The rich brother came and saw his brother's new wealth.

"How is it, Brother, that you come to have this grand party and yet last week begged at my door?" asked the rich brother.

His brother was reluctant to tell his secret, but after a few days, he told him everything. Well, his brother decided that he must have the coffee mill and offered his brother a large sum of money for it. The previously poor brother agreed to sell it to him after the summer because he figured that he would use the coffee mill to get everything he needed before then and then sell it to his brother for a fine price.

The end of summer finally arrived, and the coffee mill was sold. The other brother was in such a rush to get it home that he did not wait for directions. That night he wished for a delicious soup. His wish was answered and answered and answered, for he had not learned how to stop the mill. The soup filled all the dishes and all the pots and nearly flooded the house. He ran to his brother and demanded that he take the mill back.

The previously poor brother said he would take it back, but he would charge his brother the same price he had sold it to him

for. The brother agreed. The previously poor brother was now incredibly rich. He used his money to buy his wife a castle by the sea with gold turrets. Many people came to the castle to see who lived there. One visitor was a sea captain who saw the castle from his ship. When he arrived at the castle, he was greeted kindly and shown the now famous mill.

"If I had this mill I would no longer need to sail the seas to buy cargoes of salt," he said to his host.

"Indeed," said the previously poor brother. "I will sell the mill to you, if you so desire."

The sea captain paid a large sum for the mill and was so eager to get it to his ship (for he feared the man would change his mind) that he did not ask for directions on how to use the mill. Once the ship was far enough away from land, the captain took the mill out onto the deck.

"I wish for salt," he said to the mill. He turned the handle, and the mill began to give him salt. Since he did not know how to stop the mill, the salt kept coming. It filled the deck and then the ship. Eventually the ship cracked under the weight of the salt and sank to the bottom of the sea. The mill fell into the sea, where it is still grinding salt. And that is why the sea is salty.

Salty Water Experiment

River water that flows into the ocean is freshwater with a trace of salt and other minerals. There might be some water near the ocean that is considered *brackish*, meaning it is a mixture of both salt water and freshwater, but overall the river water has much less salt content than the ocean water. What do you think happens to the river water when it flows into the ocean? Try this experiment to see for yourself.

What You Need

- 4 clear plastic cups
- Masking tape
- Marker
- Measuring cups
- Water
- Kosher salt
- Measuring spoons
- Stirrer or spoon
- Food coloring
- Eyedropper

What You Do

1. Using the masking tape and marker, label each cup A, B, C, and D.

2. Pour 1 cup (236.58 milliliters) of water into cups A and B. Add 1 tablespoon (14.8 milliliters) of salt to cups A and B. Stir the solution until the salt dissolves. Add 2 additional teaspoons (9.9 milliliters) of salt to cup A to make an extra-salty solution.

3. Pour about ¼ cup (59.15 milliliters) of the salt solution from cup B into cup C. Add 5 drops of food coloring to cup C.

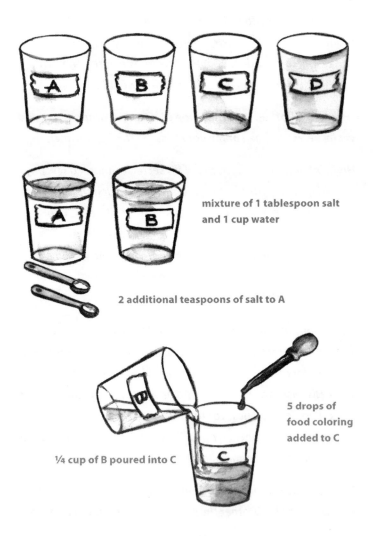

mixture of 1 tablespoon salt and 1 cup water

2 additional teaspoons of salt to A

5 drops of food coloring added to C

¼ cup of B poured into C

¼ cup of A poured into D   15 drops of C added to D

4. Pour about ¼ cup (59.15 milliliters) of the extra-salty solution from cup A into cup D.

5. Use the eyedropper to add 15 drops of the colored solution from cup C into cup D. What happens when the less salty water is introduced to the extra-salty solution? Does it float or sink? What do you think would happen if you instead did this experiment dropping the extra-salty solution into the less salty solution?

Ocean Notion

How much salt is in the ocean? If the ocean suddenly dried up and only the salt was left, there would be enough salt to give millions of boxes of salt to each person living in the United States.

Extra-salty water is denser and heavier than the less salty water and tends to sink in the ocean. Freshwater from the rivers tends to float in the ocean.

Ocean Motion

Tides are not the only cause of ocean movement. Have you ever tried to swim in the ocean? If you have, you might have felt the water pull you in a certain direction. This pull feels almost like a stream of water flowing under the waves. Actually it is. These underwater streams and rivers are called *currents*. A current can be very strong, just like a fast-moving river.

Sometimes the water that is flowing in the current is a different temperature than the water around it. Why do you think it would be warmer or colder? If you look on a weather map, you might see the direction of some of these currents. Currents take warm water toward the North and South poles and cold water toward the equator. One current that you may have heard about is the Gulf Stream. The *Gulf Stream* carries warm water from the Caribbean Sea up the eastern coast of the United States, then across the Atlantic to the west coasts of Britain and northern Europe. Without this current flowing in the ocean, much of the waters and land of the eastern United States and the coasts of Britain and northern Europe would be much colder.

Bathtub Gulf Stream

In the days of Colonial America, ships would travel and transport goods from the colonies to England and other parts of Europe. Ben Franklin began to notice that it took the sailors less time to travel from the colonies to Europe than from Europe to the colonies. He discovered that when the ships traveled to Europe they followed a current that pushed them along quickly, but on the way home the ships traveled against the current, creating a slower voyage. This current became known as the Gulf Stream.

Did you ever try to swim against a current? Is it easy or difficult? Have you ever heard someone refer to somebody as "swimming against the current"? What do you think they meant? You can create your own Gulf Stream current in your bathtub. Try this the next time you need a bath.

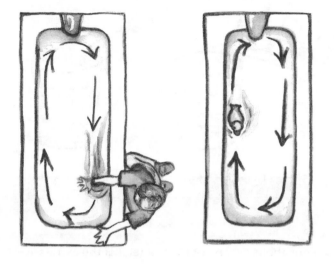

What You Need
➤ Bathtub
➤ Water
➤ Floating bathtub toy

What You Do
1. Fill the bathtub halfway and let the water settle until it's flat and calm.
2. Dip your hand into the water and begin pushing the water in one direction. You will begin to feel the water flowing around the bathtub like the Gulf Stream current.
3. Place a floating bath toy in the bathtub and continue to push the water. Which way does the bath toy travel? Try moving the toy in the opposite direction. Is it difficult? From this little experiment, which direction do you think would be easier for a boat to travel?

Making Waves

Winds blowing over the ocean create waves. The winds may create waves off the western coast of the United States, and these waves could be the same waves people will see rolling in Japan thousands of miles away!

The waves rise and fall, but the water does not really move. It follows a circular pattern. You can see this happen if you watch a bird bobbing up and down on the waves in the ocean or a lake. You will see that the bird is not carried along with the wave as the wave passes.

Slow-Motion Ocean Bottle

Waves move so fast on the ocean that it may be hard to focus on one wave, although it's fun to try. Here's a way to slow them down a bit: make your own wave.

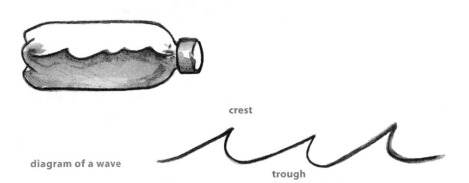

diagram of a wave — crest — trough

What You Need

- Clear 1-liter soda bottle with bottle top
- Water
- Blue food coloring
- Baby oil or cooking oil

What You Do

1. Fill half the bottle with water. Add a few drops of blue food coloring.

2. Fill the rest of the bottle with oil. Your measurements don't have to be exact. In fact, it may even work better with a little less water.

3. Screw on the bottle top tightly. Turn your bottle onto its side. Move it back and forth and watch the waves! See if you can find the crest and the trough of each wave. The *crest* is the top of the wave just before the wave falls, and the *trough* is the low part of the wave just after it's fallen.

Making More Waves

Want more natural waves? Try this. Fill a square cake pan halfway with water. Take a straw and hold it just above the water with the opening on an angle. Blow gently through the straw and watch the waves develop across the pan.

Surf's Up

You might think that the highest waves are found under the surfboards of Hawaiian surfers, but you would be wrong. The world's highest waves are found off the coast of South Africa in the area around the Alguhas Current. High waves are also found along the southwest coast of England. Can you find these spots on a map? Why do you think the waves are so high in these areas?

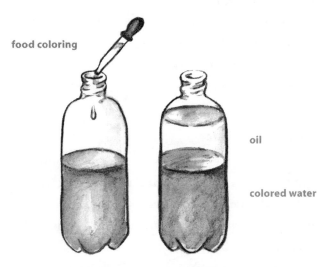

food coloring

oil

colored water

The Beaufort Scale

Wave height is determined by the strength of blowing winds, the duration of the winds, and the distance the wave travels without reaching land. The *Beaufort scale* describes the strength of sea winds. It is named after Francis Beaufort, an admiral in the British Navy in the early 1800s. The numbers on the scale range from 0, indicating a perfectly calm sea, to 12, indicating hurricane waves of 45 feet (13.72 meters) and higher. Who do you think would benefit from knowing the Beaufort scale ratings? You'll find the Beaufort scale in the dictionary. See if you can find out the Beaufort scale rating for any ocean area on a given day.

El Niño

Newspapers across the world printed front-page headlines on the fury of El Niño, which caused drought in Australia, floods in Peru, and tornadoes in Florida. In California, sea lions went hungry because ocean temperatures were too warm to support the fish they usually fed on. New York City was eight degrees warmer than usual for the month of January 1998. A blizzard dumped 22 inches (55.88 centimeters) of snow on Denver, Colorado. Storms and cold temperatures hit the southern United States. Olympic organizers worried they would not have enough snow for the Olympics in Japan, and then worried that there would be too much snow. Warm water damaged the coral reefs near the Galapagos Islands, too.

Could all these events be blamed on the flow of warm ocean water in the Pacific Ocean? Yes, the warm waters of El Niño, caused by a weakening of normal east-west trade winds, were responsible for weather changes across the globe. How do you think El Niño would affect your neighborhood? How about where you vacation?

Rave Waves

Waves can sometimes get a bit out of hand. Sometimes giant waves, called *tidal waves*, roar into a coastline. In India, tidal waves have killed many thousands of people. Tidal waves are not actually caused by tides but by underwater earthquakes and volcanic eruptions. They occur so often in the Pacific waters near Japan that the Japanese have their own name for them: *tsunami*. Can you imagine a tidal wave or tsunami as tall as a 10-story building? What precautions would need to be taken to keep an area safe from a wave that large?

Jump Right In

Now that you've explored some ocean dynamics, let's begin to explore the life in and beneath the waves. The ocean is divided into different zones or layers. The ocean surface and a bit below the surface is called the *sunlit zone*. Let's find out why.

2
Enter the Sunlit Zone

Imagine that you are diving into the deep blue ocean. You fly through the bright sunlit sky and touch down in the cool water. On your way down through the water the ocean becomes darker and you see less of your surroundings. You turn around to swim to the surface and look up. It is still dark, but as you begin to swim up toward the surface, the water becomes lighter. Soon the sun's rays are shining through the cool waves and you see fish dart by. You are now in the sunlit zone where the ocean is lit by sunlight. It is rich with life. Some sea animals drift on the waves, while others swim. On warm summer nights these waters twinkle with starlight and the glowing bodies of sea animals.

Algae, the First Link in the Ocean Food Chain

The sunlit zone supports a tremendous population of tiny algae that capture energy from the sunlight and the carbon dioxide in seawater and air. It is lucky for us that as a result, algae produce much of the world's oxygen supply.

Algae is also known as *seaweed*. The three main groups of seaweed are red, brown, and green algae. There are many animals that feed on algae. Do you think people also eat algae? Carrageenan, alginates, and beta-carotene are derived from marine algae and often end up in our food to act as stabilizers or thickeners or to add color. Carrageenan comes from red algae and is often added as a gelatin alternative, and alginates from brown algae are often used to prevent ice crystals from forming in ice cream. (Check out Chapter 4 for more about seaweed.) Beta-carotene comes from green algae. It is used as a food coloring and may also help prevent some forms of cancer.

Seaweed Snooper

Take a look through your kitchen cupboard and refrigerator. Look at the ingredients listed on the foods you eat. Do you see carrageenan listed? Maybe you'll find beta-carotene or alginate listed among the ingredients. How many products can you find that include seaweed? Hint: Look at ice cream, toothpaste, pet food, pudding, mayonnaise, and cheese.

Ocean Algae Combat Greenhouse Effect

The *greenhouse effect* is a rising in temperature across the earth caused by gases that hold the heat in the earth's atmosphere. Carbon dioxide is the primary gas responsible for this effect. Reducing the amount of carbon dioxide in the air might actually reduce the greenhouse effect.

Algae draw carbon dioxide from the air and release oxygen back into the air through the process of *photosynthesis*. Scientists are now experimenting with increasing the growth of algae in the ocean so that more carbon dioxide will be consumed. The hope is that this might be a way to combat the greenhouse effect.

Ocean Notion
Animals and plants that drift with the water are called *plankton*. The word *plankton* comes from the Greek word *planktos*, which means wandering. A good name for these critters, don't you think?

Instant Jellyfish

Jellyfish, or sea jellies, are really not fish at all. These animals drift through the sunlit zone without the backbones, gills, or scales that fish have. Instead, jellies get their name for their soft, squishy bodies, which would feel like liquid-filled plastic bags. And they *are* liquid-filled—sea jellies are made up of about 95 percent water! There's not much you need to make your own jellyfish model at home. Here's how to do it.

What You Need
- 2 clear plastic bags
- Water
- Food coloring
- Bag tie

What You Do

1. To make the body, fill one plastic bag half full with water and add a few drops of food coloring.

food coloring

2. Add just a little water to the second bag and push it inside the first to create the stomach of the jelly.

3. Tie the two bags together with a bag tie and carefully turn the bags over. Tuck in the corners of the bags.

4. Place your jelly model in a basin of water and watch it float!

tied

The Sting Solution

Jellies catch their food using their stinging tentacles. As they float along they spread out their tentacles like an electric net. Tiny plankton and other small sea animals swim or float into the net. Jellies then paralyze their victim with stinging cells, called *nematocysts*, that act as tiny harpoons.

Most jellies are not dangerous to people. Only a few sport enough stinging capability to make them dangerous, even deadly, to people. If you are, however, swimming in the company of jellies, be aware that they do not sting people on purpose, but a brush against one can result in a painful sting. Believe it or not, a dead jellyfish still sports a powerful sting. In fact, even a broken tentacle can still sting as long as it is wet. The good news is that not all jellies sting!

Here's your chance to play scientist and see if you can come up with a way to protect swimmers from the sting of sea jellies.

What You Need
→ Paper
→ Pencil
→ A few friends

What You Do
1. Think about products you use that help protect you from other stings, such as types of insect repellents. Write these down. How do these items protect you? Do they discourage the insect from biting you, or do they form a barrier so that the sting can't reach you?

2. Talk about ways that swimmers come in contact with jellyfish. What are some products that might help protect swimmers from the sting of sea jellies? Think of items that might discourage jellies from coming near swimmers and items that would protect the skin of swimmers who come in contact with jellies.

3. Do library or Internet research to discover products currently on the market to protect swimmers from jellies. Did you come up with any product ideas that are similar to the products currently on the market? Any new products?

A Jelly Sandwich?

Not all animals are frightened off by the sting of a sea jelly. Some creatures, such as sunfish, seabirds, and sea turtles, actually find the sea jelly a simply delicious meal!

Free-Floating Jellies

Make these tiny jellies to hang everywhere you need a little bit of ocean in your life. Keep in mind that many jellies are tiny, but some can have a bell that is six feet (1.8 meters) across. Measure out six feet on your floor to see just how big some jellies can grow.

What You Need

Makes 12 jellies

- Egg carton
- Scissors
- Iridescent and colored tissue paper
- Ruler
- Pencil
- White craft glue
- Ribbons, cut into six- to eight-inch (15.24 to 20.32 centimeters) lengths
- 12 6-inch (15.24 centimeters) pipe cleaners
- Sewing needle
- Fishing line

What You Do

1. Use the scissors to cut out each cup from the egg carton. Cut off the edges of each cup to form a rough circle. Turn the cups over to create the bell of your jelly.

2. For each jelly's bell, cut two 6-inch (15.24 centimeters) squares of tissue paper, one iridescent and one solid color.

3. Dab some glue on the top of the egg cup. Adhere the center of the solid-colored square of tissue paper to the center of the cup. Apply more glue to the center of the solid-colored tissue paper and then add the iridescent tissue paper layer on top of the first.

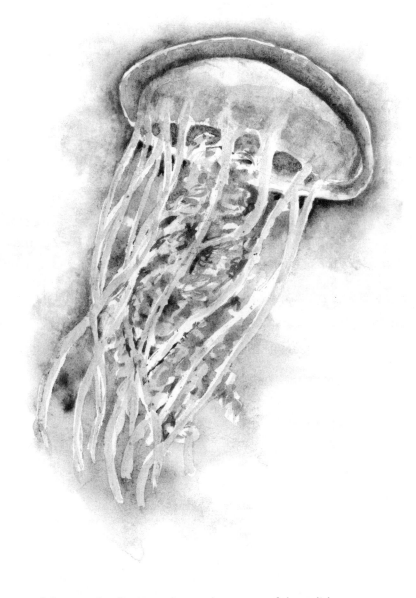

4. Curl the ribbons by pulling them across the scissors or another flat surface. This will create the tentacles for your jelly.

5. Attach three to seven ribbon tentacles to the inside of the bell with glue.

6. Form a ring out of a pipe cleaner and place it around the bottom of the bell, holding the tissue paper in place. Pull out the tissue paper around the pipe cleaner enough to form a round jelly skirt.

7. Thread the needle with the fishing line and pierce the top of the jelly. Bring the fishing line back up through the top of the jelly and tie a knot. Your little jelly is all set to hang.

Ocean Notion

You have probably heard of a gaggle of geese, herd of cattle, or flock of birds. What do you think a group of jellies is called? A group of jellies is called a *smack*.

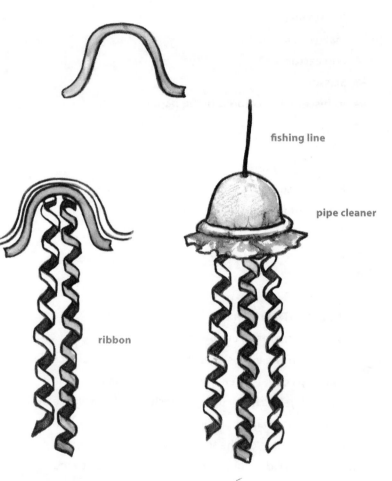

fishing line

pipe cleaner

glue

iridescent tissue paper (second)

solid-colored tissue paper (first)

egg cup for jelly bell

ribbon

The Turtles of the Sea

Have you ever seen or touched a turtle that lives in a freshwater pond or woodland area? The turtles of the sea have many similarities and many differences with these turtles. They are all reptiles. Reptiles all have scaly skin, a three-chambered heart, and lungs to breath air. Like many reptiles, all turtles lay eggs. All turtles have a shell. The top of the shell is called the *carapace* and the bottom is called the *plastron*. All sea turtles, except the leatherbacks, have scales, called *scutes*, that cover their shell.

There are eight species of sea turtles. The green sea turtle and the black sea turtle eat only ocean greens. You could say they are the only vegetarians in the bunch.

The others enjoy eating jellies, shrimp, mollusks, sponges, squid, and other seafood.

Sea turtles have been swimming in the oceans for millions of years and have been the subjects of legends, myths, and creation stories. For example, the Iroquois believed that in the beginning there was no world as we know it, but there was a great ocean. It was into this ocean that a woman from the Sky-World fell. A great sea turtle agreed to receive the woman on his back. It is on this great sea turtle's back that the earth was formed as the woman walked around and around in the direction of the sun.

Compare Weights

How big do you think a sea turtle is compared to you? Let's do an experiment. We'll use the loggerhead sea turtle for this experiment. It is about 32 to 41 inches (81.28 to 104.14 centimeters) long and weighs about 146 to 223 pounds (66.2 to 101.2 kilograms).

What You Need

- Scale
- Paper
- Pencil
- Calculator

What You Do

1. Use the scale to find out how much you weigh.
2. Write down your weight and the weight of a few of your friends.
3. How many kids does it take to weigh as much as a loggerhead? Let's find out by first finding out the average weight of your friends. Add up all of the weights of your friends on the calculator. After you have the total weight, divide this by the number of friends you weighed. This will give you their average weight.
4. Divide the average weight of a loggerhead—about 185 pounds (83.91 kilograms)—by the average weight of your friends. This will tell you the number of kids it would take to equal the weight of a loggerhead.

More Turtle Fun

Imagine the weight of a turtle compacted into about three feet (91.44 centimeters)! A leatherback sea turtle weighs the most of all sea turtles. It is about four to six feet (121.92 to182.88 centimeters) long and can weigh up to 1,000 pounds (453.6 kilograms)! How many kids would it take to weigh as much as a leatherback?

Sea Turtles in Peril

There are many threats to sea turtles. In fact, most sea turtles are now listed as a threatened or an endangered species.

Although the turtle populations are in serious danger, people can still make a difference in their survival. This was demonstrated when a serious threat to turtle populations was virtually eliminated recently. Many sea turtles were being caught in fishing nets. The turtles were unable to escape when they were caught and were drowning in the fishing nets. Thanks to a new net design and recent laws, sea turtles are now able to escape and swim away.

Unfortunately, there are still other threats. Sea turtles are suffering from a loss of habitat. A sea turtle will only lay eggs on the beach where it was born. But many of these beaches are now gone or are populated by nearby resorts. After a turtle lays its eggs in the sand, the young must independently find their way back to the ocean. Hotel lights often guide the young turtles in the wrong direction. The people of Sanibel Island, Florida, along with other communities where sea turtles nest, are protecting their sea turtles by posting lighting restrictions and other laws to protect the egg-laying turtles.

There are also offshore threats from within the water, although the turtle does not have many natural predators in the ocean. The key word there is *natural*. Boats, an unnatural predator, can be a danger to sea turtles. When a fast-moving boat hits the shell of a turtle, the turtle can become paralyzed. Unable to swim, the turtles often die. Some are lucky enough to be found and brought to Sea World or another rehabilitative center. Many of these turtles survive but become floaters, meaning that when their shell heals, an air pocket forms underneath that prevents them from diving underwater. It's like swimming with a buoy on your back. Unable to feed underwater on their own, these turtles end up in marine parks.

What else do you think can be done to protect the turtles and their beaches?

Things You Can Do to Help Protect Turtles

You can help sea turtles even if you don't live near the ocean. Here's how.

1. Let people know that helium balloons that are released outdoors often end up in the ocean where sea turtles mistake them for yummy jellies. They often eat them and then die.

2. Encourage your family and friends to use organic or biodegradable garden products instead of toxic chemicals. Chemicals from groundwater eventually end up in the ocean.

3. Reduce the amount of plastic your family uses. It can end up in the ocean as dumped garbage. Use canvas bags to bring home groceries and reusable plastic containers to store leftovers.

Archie Carr, Ocean Hero

Probably the most successful crusader to address the plight of the sea turtles was Archie Carr. He was born in 1909. When Archie was a boy, he kept all kinds of snakes, lizards, and turtles at his home in Georgia. As he grew older, his love of the outdoors was matched by his love of the written and spoken word.

He won the O. Henry Award for a short story and the John Burroughs Medal of the American Museum of Natural History for nature writing. During his career he published 10 books and 120 scientific papers.

He earned his doctorate in zoology from the University of Florida and spent the rest of his years as a teacher and biologist. During the 1960s, Dr. Carr obtained a grant from the Office of Naval Research to study sea turtle migration and navigation. Thanks to military transport he was able to fly anywhere in the world that the United States military flew in order to study the sea turtles. His studies took him to the Gulf of Mexico, Central America, South America, the Caribbean, Australia, Papua New Guinea, and Africa. He became respected throughout the world for his sea turtle research.

But Dr. Carr didn't stop there. His research led him to the discovery that sea turtle populations were in drastic need of conservation, so he began to address the plight of the sea turtle as well as continue his research. Dr. Carr's longtime conservation efforts became a reality with the development of the Tortuego National Park in Costa Rica. The Caribbean Conservation Corporation was created to support the park, which today is still a leader in sea turtle research and conservation.

Archie Carr died in 1987, but he left behind a tremendous contribution to sea turtle conservation.

Urashima Taro, a Japanese Legend

This is a portion of the legend of Urashima Taro that features a sea turtle. (Complete versions of this legend can be found in collections of Japanese fairy tales.)

Long ago in Japan there lived a poor but kind fisherman named Urashima Taro. One day as he was walking along the beach with his nets, he came across some boys throwing sticks and broken shells at a gigantic sea turtle that was making its way back to the sea.

"Stop!" he cried. "Stop! Don't you know that every living thing on this earth is your brother or sister, and you should act with kindness? What's more, the turtle, the messenger of the Dragon King who lives under the sea, is said to live 10,000 years. If you kill something that might have lived so many years, the loss of all those years will pile up against you. It is dangerous and wrong."

At this, Urashima Taro gave the boys some coins to go away and leave the turtle alone. The turtle crawled back into the sea and disappeared under the waves.

Urashima took out his boat and began to fish. The warm sun and gentle rocking of the boat soon put Urashima Taro to sleep. When he woke he saw before him a beautiful woman rising out of the waves.

"Urashima Taro, I am the daughter of the Dragon King from under the sea. Your kind deed to my father's messenger, the turtle, made my father very pleased." With that she gave Urashima a great treasure.

What would you have done if you were Urashima Taro and saw the boys throwing sticks and shells at a giant sea turtle? Why is it important to act kindly to sea turtles and other creatures? In the tale, Urashima Taro says that sea turtles are said to live 10,000 years. Do you think that turtles can live that long? How long do turtles live? You may be surprised at the answer.

Flying-Fish Kite

Believe it or not, flying fish are not a circus act, but real fish. Flying fish live in and out of the sunlit zone in tropical and subtropical waters. Rather than actually flying, they do sort of a hang-gliding feat. They have the same number of fins as other fish, but their fins are elongated to provide them with just enough lift to keep them airborne when they jump. They can actually rise to a height of 50 feet above the surface of the water, provided they catch a strong gust of wind. Now that's a pretty good escape from a hungry bluefish! Unfortunately, in escaping their enemies they sometimes slam into unsuspecting boats.

It's easy to make your own fish fly through the air just like a flying fish. Here's how.

What You Need
- Tissue paper
- Scissors
- Markers
- White craft glue
- Thin florist wire
- Thin string
- Tape

What You Do
1. Cut out the shape of a fish from two sheets of tissue paper.

2. Using markers, add eyes and any other decorations to your fish.

3. Glue the two sides together, leaving the mouth unglued, by running a thin line of glue around the edges.

4. Make a circle out of thin wire.

5. Attach two strings to the wire and place the wire inside the mouth.

6. Tape the mouth shut. Let the fish dry, then head outside to catch a breeze.

Get Your Feet Wet

If you are lucky, you might catch a glimpse of a flying fish, sea turtle, or jellyfish from the bow of a boat, but there are also many other areas for you to explore if you are willing to get your feet wet. Let's start right on the beach.

glue

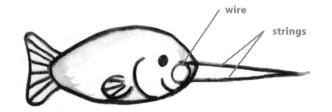

wire

strings

Explore 3
Sea Gardens
and Tide Pools

Have you ever walked along a beach at low tide? Or worn snorkel gear and examined a coral reef with flippers on your feet? If you have, then you know that you don't have to travel far out into the sea to find hundreds of creatures awaiting your discovery. Within an easy reach of the shoreline, there are reefs that parade more colors than a summer garden in full bloom and pools that become nurseries for many sea creatures. The creatures you can find in these places are sometimes mysterious, often shy, but always a marvel to watch.

Universe in a Puddle

Between high and low tides, water collects in sand and rocky depressions along the coastline. At first glance it might seem that nothing is there but clear water and some seaweed, but if you look carefully you will see many creatures crawling and swimming about in this mini-ocean world called a *tide pool*.

Watch closely and a plantlike anemone moves its tentacles. A small shell on the sand below starts to move, and soon you may even see it begin to feed on the anemone's tentacles. Anemones may look like flowers to us, but they are really animals. It's possible that the anemone you see is close to 75 years old because some of them live that long.

What else do you think lives in the tide pools? In a large tide pool there can be 600 different species of plants and animals. It's amazing, but true!

An Oasis Under Siege

Tidal pools are often compared to mini aquariums, but these are not like the peaceful aquariums you might have in your house. Inside these aquariums is a constant battle between life and death. Many creatures that live in tide pools find themselves underwater, then out of the water, then underwater, then back out of the water as the tide moves in and out about every 13 hours. What do you think these creatures do to survive these long periods without water? Some move underneath rocks to help them keep moist and cool and out of the hot sun. Others are able to travel below the surface of the sand. Crabs wedge themselves between rocks. Still others close up their shells when the conditions are too harsh.

What are some of the harsh conditions that these creatures must survive other than lack of water? Well, the temperature of the water that remains is subject to the heat of the sun and can even reach 100 degrees Fahrenheit (38 degrees Celsius), which is dangerous to most ocean life. With the hot sun comes the evaporation of water from the tide pool. Not only is this dangerous because of the water that is lost, but a greater amount of ocean salt is left behind as well. The saltwater that is left creates a pool that could be many more times as salty as normal ocean water, which could be a major problem to ocean life.

Here's another problem for tidal pool inhabitants. The tide that rushes into the pool brings with it life-giving oxygen and food but also crashing waves that can create forces that are equivalent to 30 times the pressure of a human foot. Only the strongest and hardiest of critters can withstand these types of conditions.

Ocean Notion

"It is advisable to look from a tide pool to the stars and then back to the tide pool again," wrote author John Steinbeck. What do you think he meant? Think about it.

Make a Water Snooper

If you are planning a visit to the seashore, bring along a water snooper to examine the tidal pools that you find.

What You Need

- Empty coffee can
- Can opener
- Clear plastic wrap
- Large rubber band
- A grown-up to assist

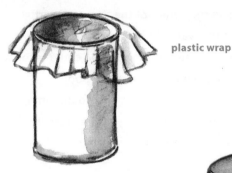

plastic wrap

rubber band

What You Do

1. Ask a grown-up to open up the closed end of an empty coffee can with a can opener.

2. Wash the can completely and stretch the plastic wrap across one end.

3. Wrap the rubber band around the can to hold the plastic wrap in place.

4. Walk gently to a tide pool. Be sure to watch where you step. Many tide pools suffer from people trampling on them. When you reach a pool, place the covered end of the snooper gently in the water. Look through the snooper into the water. What do you see? How many different creatures can you spot with your snooper?

Take the Tide Pool Challenge

Put on your marine biologist hat for this challenge. Your assignment is to record the changes in a tide pool over the course of a day. Be prepared to get wet and spend the day at the beach.

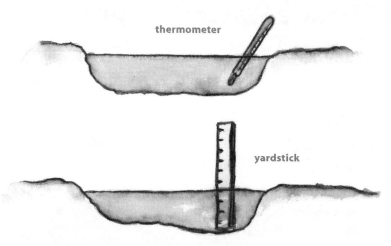

thermometer

yardstick

What You Need
➡ Paper
➡ Pencil
➡ Thermometer
➡ Yardstick
➡ Watch

What To Do

1. Locate a tide pool on the beach. Start your record chart with the time of day and the location of the tide pool. Use the record chart below as your guide.

2. Place a thermometer in the pool and record the temperature of the water.

3. Place a yardstick in the center of the tide pool and measure the depth of the water. Record this measurement. Can you think of any other measurements you could record? Write down any creatures you see in the tide pool.

4. Visit the tide pool again in an hour. Record the time, temperature, and depth again. Have any of the measurements changed? Write down any new creatures you have found as well.

5. Visit the tide pool every hour after that during your day at the beach and record your measurements. Did you write down a list of creatures that you saw in the tide pool? What have you observed during the day? If possible, visit the tide pool on another day and take additional measurements.

6. Take a look at your measurements. Did you detect any patterns in your findings? What did you discover? Present your findings to your friends or classmates.

Time	Temperature	Depth	Creatures Seen	Other Observations
10 A.M.				
11 A.M.				
12 P.M.				
1 P.M.				
2 P.M.				
3 P.M.				
4 P.M.				
5 P.M.				

Introducing the Real Star of the Tidal Pool—The Starfish!

The popular starfish is truly the star performer of the tide pool. Not only can it "see" with its arms, it can spit out its stomach and re-grow body parts through the process of *regeneration*. This bottom dweller has style!

Starfish aren't really fish, so to call them starfish is a little odd. Their shape really supports the name that scientists prefer to call them—sea stars. They belong to the same club—*echinoderms*, or spiny-skinned critters—as sea urchins and sand dollars.

Sea stars have no top or bottom. They can move in any direction, but unlike humans, they do not use muscles to help them move. Sea stars use a hydraulic system. Flip a sea star over and you will find hundreds of little tube feet lining its arms. Each tube has a suction point. The sea star can control the suction in its tube feet by changing the water pressure in each tube. The tubes are then used to move the star along. When the tube of a starfish arm comes in contact with a solid surface, it adheres to the surface, and the rest of the starfish is drawn to the point that is attached.

Most starfish have five arms. At the end of each of its arms is an eye-spot that is sensitive to light. Some are attracted to light areas, while others like to stay in the shadows. In this way sea stars are able to see with their arms.

Sea stars use their entire bodies when they eat. Their favorite food is shellfish, specifically mussels, oysters, and similar creatures. These shellfish are called *bivalves*. They have two shells that remain tightly closed to the starfish. In order to eat them, the starfish must get inside the shells, and the sea star uses its entire body to do this. The starfish uses its arms and tube feet to clamp around the shells and pry them open a tiny bit. It then spits its stomach out of its mouth and into this tiny opening. The digestive juices of the stomach then go to work, turning the body of the shellfish into liquid. The starfish arms are lined with tiny hairs, called *cilia*, that lead the liquid back to the mouth of the starfish. This process takes a long time for the starfish to complete and often leaves the starfish vulnerable to predators for a long while. Pretty gruesome, huh?

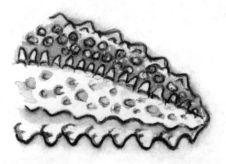

The Story of the Sea Star

There are many versions of this popular fable, but all impart the same message.

One day a man went down to the beach to fish. He cast his line out into the waves and sat down on a rock. Out of the corner of his eye he saw a young girl at the other end of the beach. Her hair was flying in the wind and her arms were flailing about. He wondered what she was doing.

As the girl came closer to the man he could see that she was continually reaching down into the sand, picking something up, and gently tossing it into the sea.

"Hi there!" he called as she came closer. "What are you picking up?"

The young girl opened up her hand to show the man the starfish she held. She then proceeded to throw it back to the waves.

"There are starfish up and down this beach," said the man. "There are just too many; you can't make a difference."

She picked up another, threw it in, and replied, "I made a difference to that one, didn't I?"

Got Milk?

If cookies and milk are your thing, this starfish will surely interest you. The Chocolate Chip Sea Star is a starfish with a lot of bite. The dark chocolate-colored "chips" on this sea star are actually clusters of jaws that help deter predators. This is definitely one chocolate chip you don't want to bite into!

Ocean Notion
Echinoderm comes from the Greek word *echinos*, which means "hedgehog." Have you ever seen a spiny-skinned hedgehog? Touch a starfish or sea urchin and decide if hedgehog skin is a good description for these critters.

Super Starfish

Here's how you can create your own tide pool superstar!

What You Need

- Oak tag or other card stock
- Pencil
- Scissors
- Paper plate
- Paint
- Bubble wrap
- White craft glue
- Sand
- Needle
- String

What You Do

1. Using your pencil, draw a starfish on the oak tag. Remember most starfish have five arms.
2. Cut out your starfish shape.

3. Pour some paint onto the paper plate. Dip a piece of bubble wrap into the paint and dab it over the starfish you just cut out. This will create the tube feet of your starfish. Allow the paint to dry.
4. Turn the starfish over and, using your finger, spread the craft glue over the unpainted side of the starfish.
5. Sprinkle the sand over the glue and pat it down with your hand. When your starfish is completed, poke a hole in one of the arms with the needle and tie a string through it so that you can hang it up. Make a few more starfish and you can create a starfish mobile.

The Coral Reef

If the tide pool can be compared to an aquarium, then the *coral reef* is the blooming garden outside. It is alive with brightly colored fish, coral of all shapes and sizes, and thousands of other sea creatures.

It is sometimes hard to believe that the reef corals that look like feathers and leafy fronds are really animals and not plants. The coral reefs are actually built by tiny animals called *polyps*. These polyps extract lime from the seawater around them, combine it with carbon dioxide, and make a form of calcium called *aragonite*. This mineral, the rock that is created from it, and the polyps are all called coral. There is an interesting twist, however: within the coral polyps are tiny plants. These tiny plants live within the tissue of most corals. They help the coral polyps to create their limestone skeletons. So, coral is an animal, but an animal that has plants living within it. Amazing, but true!

There are corals found in all of the oceans of the world, but the stony corals that create large reefs are warm water corals. They need temperatures of 68 to 82 degrees Farenheit (20 to 28 degrees Celsius) to thrive. That explains why reefs are scattered throughout the tropical and subtropical oceans within 30 degrees north and south of the equator.

There are three types of reefs: barrier, fringing, and atoll. *Barrier reefs*, like the Great Barrier Reef off the

Ocean Notion
The coral reefs located off Mexico's Yucatan Peninsula and nearby Belize and Grand Cayman Island are some of the most frequently visited reefs in the world because of their beauty. Like all reefs, they are rich in marine life. In fact, more than one quarter of the world's estimated 15,000 marine algae species and 500,000 marine animal species call coral reefs their home.

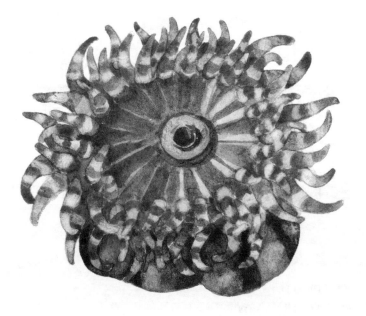

anemone. The anemone doesn't sting the clownfish because it thinks that the clownfish is just a part of itself.

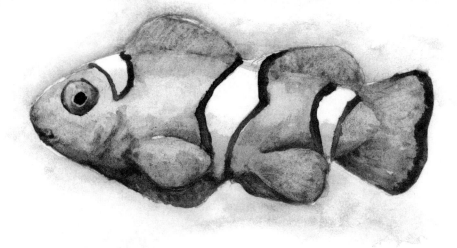

coast of Australia, are found offshore. *Fringing reefs* are also found offshore but closer to the shorelines of islands and continents. *Atolls* are, in a way, coral islands. They form near a volcanic island that has become submerged in the ocean.

Clowning Around the Reef

Amidst the poisonous tentacles of the reef's sea anemones lives a brightly colored fish that swims freely without getting stung. It is the clownfish. Why doesn't it get stung like other fish? The clownfish has a special layer of mucus, just like the mucus that covers the

Cleaner-Fish Challenge

The little blue and yellow cleaner wrasse (pronounced ras) fish is one of 600 species of wrasse that inhabit the ocean. It makes its home in coral reefs around the world, where it sets up its own "dental office" for the fish of the reef. Fish actually line up at the wrasse's dental office to be "cleaned." The wrasse removes parasites and loose skin from fins and gills. It will even go inside the mouth of its patient to clean between the teeth of the patient fish. The wrasse enjoys a yummy meal, and the cleaned fish leave free of parasites and loose skin. Learn more about cleaner fish with this fun challenge.

fish

fish

timekeeper

cleaner fish

What You Need

➤ 4 players

➤ 30 small stickers

➤ Stopwatch

What You Do

1. Choose two players to be the fish, one player to be the cleaner fish, and one player to keep time.

2. Place 15 stickers all over the shirts of the two fish.

3. In a 30-second time period, have one of the fish remove the stickers from his or her own shirt. Let the cleaner fish remove the stickers from the other fish.

4. At the end of 30 seconds, compare the two shirts of the fish players. Which one has fewer stickers left? Think about how cleaner fish take off bits of dirt and parasites on fish.

5. Talk together about people who help clean and groom other people, such as dentists and hairdressers. Why do we need other people to keep us clean and healthy?

Tomorrow's Reefs

We have a lot to do to protect the future of the world's reefs. The rapid growth in population in tropical countries has taken its toll on the ocean's coral reefs. As land is cleared for housing and farms, silt and topsoil run into the ocean, covering and killing the coral. The increase in shell and fish collecting has caused damage as well. All different kinds of ocean pollution, including garbage and pesticides, poison the live coral. Sewage and fertilizers that flow into the ocean waters create an abundance of algae, which can smother the coral.

Even so, not all reef destruction is caused by humans. Large sections of the Great Barrier Reef are being eaten away by the "crown of thorns" starfish. This multirayed starfish has spines that resemble a sea urchin. It can be about 15 inches (38.1 centimeters) across— larger than a dinner plate! This starfish sucks in the living coral polyp, digests it, and leaves behind only the coral skeleton, which is later invaded by algae.

Ocean Notion
Scientists are exploring the bacteria in coral reef sponges for naturally occuring antibiotics. Just think, there may be a time when your doctor prescribes an antibiotic that was developed from a coral reef sponge! Who knows what other cures may be found in the ocean in the future.

Ten Things You Can Do to Help Save Coral Reefs

Does the future look bleak for the coral reefs? Some may say it does, but others are working hard to keep the reefs clean and healthy. Even if you do not live near a coral reef, there are things that you can do to help keep them healthy.

1. Visit a coral reef on vacation. Strap on a snorkel and enjoy the reef's beauty, while abiding by the rules and regulations to keep it healthy. Seeing it firsthand will help you appreciate its beauty.

2. Learn more about coral reefs. Share what you learn with your family and friends.

3. Join a local aquarium. Ask if any part of your donation contributes to reef protection.

4. Don't pollute.

5. Don't buy coral products.

6. Recycle.

7. Conserve water. This means less waste water will reach the ocean.

8. Shop wisely for aquarium fish. Ask how the fish were collected or bred before you purchase any for your tank.

9. Surf the Internet for Web sites that will provide you with information about reef protection.

10. Ask your parents to buy natural pesticides and fertilizers instead of ones that are chemically treated.

Shoebox Reef

Here's how to create your own reef complete with your favorite reef creatures.

What You Need
- Shoebox with lid
- Scissors
- Blue tissue paper
- Pencil
- White craft glue
- Card stock or oak tag in a variety of colors
- Shells (optional)

What You Do

1. Poke a hole in the shoebox lid with the scissors, about ½ inch (1.27 centimeters) from the edge of the lid. Now cut a window in the lid, leaving a ½-inch (1.27-centimeter) margin around all the edges.

2. Place the lid on the tissue paper and trace around it with a pencil. Cut out the completed rectangle and glue it to the underside of the lid to cover the window. Place the lid aside.

3. Using the scissors, cut a small peephole in the center of a small end of the shoebox.

4. Now it's time to create your reef. Place the lid gently on the box and take a peek inside through the peephole. The blue tissue paper will let just enough light in to make your reef appear to be under the blue ocean waves. Start picturing your reef inside the box. Glue some blue paper or tissue paper to the inside of the box to cover the cardboard.

peephole

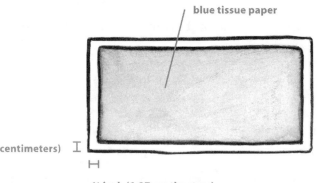

blue tissue paper

½ inch (1.27 centimeters)

½ inch (1.27 centimeters)

that it will be able to stand in your box after it is glued to the bottom.

6. Glue the first piece of coral toward the front of your box, the second in the middle, and the third in the back. Look through the peephole while you position them so that you can make sure that you can see them when they are glued.

7. After you have positioned your coral, cut out your reef creatures from the colored card stock. They can be glued to the back wall of your box, the sides, and the coral. You can even add some shells to the floor of your box to make it look like the sea floor.

8. Place the lid back onto the box when you have finished. Take a peek through the peephole. How does your reef look?

Beyond the Reef

Take a voyage beyond the reefs to underwater forests and into the world of ocean myths and mermaids.

5. Choose the color of card stock you want to use for your coral. Coral comes in many different shapes. Cut out at least three coral shapes to fit inside your box. Be sure they will fit with the box lid on. Fold down the bottom of the coral so

Search Out
Ocean Meadows
and Mermaids

Imagine a forest under the ocean where large plants grow upward toward the sunlight and fish swim in between the green fronds. Imagine vast areas of grasses beneath the waves that rival any prairie meadow. These are the places of manatees and sea otters, of blue-eyed scallops and sea urchins. Come explore these shallow, sunny places where mermaid legends are born. You will be amazed at what you find.

Kelp Seaweed Seascape

In the shallow, cool, open coastal waters of the Pacific Northwest, Cape Cod, and Long Island grow forests of giant kelp. Like coral reefs, the kelp forests occur at depths of about 98 feet (30 meters) or so, but unlike the coral they do not require warm tropical water. These huge fronds of seaweed hold fast to the rocky ocean floor. They can grow 18 inches (45.72 centimeters) per day and reach lengths of over 200 feet (60.96 meters).

Like their counterparts on land, kelp forests change with the seasons. During the winter months the rough waves wreak havoc on the fronds, tearing them from their rocks and casting them onto the beach. The forest becomes thinner. New growth in the spring begins to fill in the kelp forest gaps, just as trees on land sprout leaves each spring.

Kelps resemble land plants but have many different structures. Many land plants have leaves. Kelp plants have *blades* that use the sun's energy for making food, just like leaves. At the bottom of each blade is a round, air-filled sac called a *float*. It helps keep the kelp toward the surface. The portion of the kelp that looks like a stem is called a *stipe*. Together the blade, float, and stipe make up the part of the kelp called the *frond*.

Kelps do not have roots. Instead of roots, they each have a *holdfast*. The holdfast, at the base of the plant, looks a lot like a root, but unlike a root, the holdfast does not bring nutrients and water to the plant. It does, however, hold the kelp in place so that the currents don't take it away, just as roots hold the land plants in the earth.

You can create a kelp forest seascape to hang on the wall.

What You Need

- Watercolor paper or heavy white paper
- Green crayons or pastels
- Blue watercolor paint
- Paintbrush

What You Do

1. Draw large fronds of kelp on the paper with green crayons. Try experimenting with different green crayons to give the seaweed a more realistic look. Vary the pressure you apply to the crayons to create different shades.

2. Paint over the entire paper with the blue watercolor paint. You'll find that the blue paint will cover all the areas that weren't colored to create a real ocean water look.

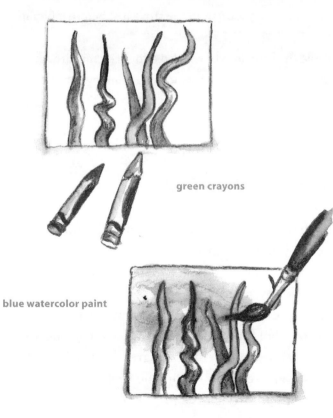

green crayons

blue watercolor paint

Munching Otters Save Kelp Forests!

Sea otters, unlike the freshwater otters, rarely leave the water. You have probably seen pictures of them floating on their backs munching their latest meal. Their love of yummy sea urchins and tasty abalone help preserve the giant kelp forests. The sea urchins and abalone graze on the kelp holdfasts, and since otters keep the sea urchin and abalone populations in check, they can't destroy the kelp forests.

In the 1800s hunting almost eliminated the sea otters from the California coast. The sea urchins and abalone populations increased and nearly destroyed the kelp forests. Now the sea otters are back, and that's a very good thing.

Make Miso Soup with Kelp

Like other seaweed, kelp is very nutritious. It's a common ingredient in many Japanese recipes. It is high in iron, iodine, calcium, vitamin C, and vitamins B_1 and B_2. Here's a simple Japanese recipe that uses kelp.

What You Need

- Water
- Large bowl
- 2 to 3 sheets kelp (about a handful; found in health food stores packaged under the name Wakame)
- Soup pot
- Stove
- Measuring spoon
- Miso (either instant or fresh)
- Soup ladle
- Sliced mushrooms, scallions, or tofu for garnish
- A grown-up to assist

What You Do

1. Take a piece of kelp out of the package and place it in a bowl of warm water. The dried kelp will soften in a few minutes.

Miso

2. After a few minutes, pick up the softened kelp and take a look at it. What does if feel like? Can you picture it growing in the ocean?

3. With your fingers, pull off any hard stems. (Do you remember what the stems are called?) Tear the kelp into small pieces and rinse.

4. Pour 4 cups (.95 liters) of water into a pot. Ask a grown-up to place the pot on the stove.

5. Add 3 tablespoons (44.4 milliliters) of fresh miso or a package of instant miso.

6. Add the kelp to the mixture and heat over a medium flame. Remove the soup from the stove just before it begins to boil.

7. Ladle the soup into bowls and add sliced mushrooms, scallions, or tofu for garnish. Enjoy your yummy soup of the sea!

Ocean Meadows

Just as they do on land, grasses flower and grow beneath the ocean water, forming large meadows. These ocean meadows provide a home for many fish, shellfish, and animals. Many marine animals, such as the manatee and green sea turtle, feed on the grasses. The grasses also help to hold the sediment of the sea floor together, preventing erosion, just like land grasses. And like other plants, sea grasses use sunlight and carbon dioxide and release oxygen through the process of photosynthesis.

People take in the oxygen and release carbon dioxide when they breathe. Oxygen is important for all of us in the world.

Manatees Are Gentle Giants

The large, slow-moving manatees live in the warm Florida waters where the sea grass grows. Commonly referred to as sea cows because of their grazing behavior, these huge animals average 1,000 pounds (453.6 kilograms), reach over 10 feet (3.048 meters) in length, and resemble a large, gray blimp. They have folds of leathery skin, tiny eyes, stubby front flippers, and a huge beaverlike tail that helps move them in the water. Manatees tend to be shy, but many do seem genuinely happy to encounter swimming people and dogs.

Because manatees move so slowly through the water and are friendly, they have had some problems in heavily populated Florida waters. They encounter the most problems when they surface for air and are not fast enough to move out of the way of oncoming, fast-moving boats. Many manatees have been hurt by boat propellers. Often they are scarred, and many have not survived.

Many environmental groups have gotten involved in the plight of the manatee. Some feel that the only way to save the manatee is to discourage any interaction between humans and manatees. Others feel that people need to be made aware of manatees, and by seeing and interacting with them, they will want to protect them. What do you think?

Manatees Versus Cows

How do a manatee and a cow really compare? Make lists to compare their weight, size, foods they eat, and any other characteristics you can think of. Are they more alike or different than you thought?

Ocean Notion
Manatees belong to the order Sirenia. The name of the order is derived from Greek mythology. Sirens were mythical creatures that had the body of a bird and the head of a beautiful woman. They were said to lure ships onto the rocks with their magical songs. Why do you suppose manatees are named after these mythical creatures?

Mermaid Mania

For many centuries there have been tales and reported sightings of mermaids. In fact, there is even an entry on mermaids in Pliny's *The Natural History*, written before Pliny's death in A.D. 79. He wrote, "As for the mermaids called Nereides, it is no fabulous tale that goeth of them: for look at how painters draw them. . . . For such a mermaid was seen and beheld plainly upon the same coast near to the shore." Much later, in 1625, explorer Henry Hudson wrote an entry in his journal about mermaids. "This evening (June 15) one of our company, looking overboard, saw a mermaid, and calling up some of the company to see her, on more of the crew came up, and by that time she was come close to the ship's side, looking earnestly on the men."

Why do you think so many sailors have spied mermaids throughout history? Scientists have tried to explain away the sightings of mermaids with the theory that perhaps sailors mistook sightings of manatees for lovely mermaids. Take a look at a picture of a manatee and a picture of a mermaid. What do you think? Would you mistake a manatee for a mermaid if you saw one swimming beside your ship?

Ocean Notion
Have you seen any mermaid movies? Which is your favorite? Look in the resources section at the back of this book for a list of movies you might enjoy.

Mermaid Shadow-Puppet Theater

Shadow puppets have been around for as long as mermaid tales, so use this mermaid shadow puppet to tell your favorite mermaid story to your friends.

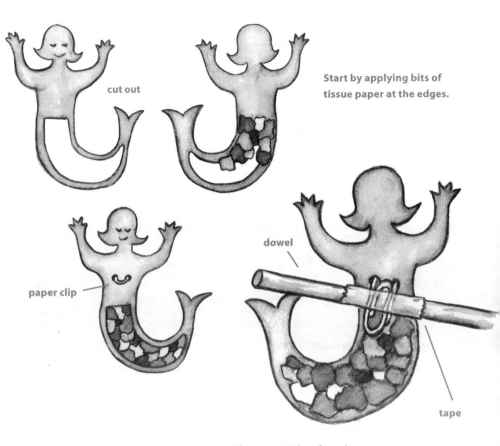

cut out

Start by applying bits of tissue paper at the edges.

paper clip

dowel

tape

THE PUPPET

What You Need

- Card stock
- Pencil
- Ruler
- Scissors
- Colored tissue paper or colored wax paper
- Glue stick
- Paper clip
- 1 12-inch (30.48 centimeters) wooden dowel ¼ to ½ inch (.64 to 1.27 centimeters) in diameter
- Tape
- A grown-up to assist

What You Do

1. Draw a mermaid on the card stock. Make sure that you do not make her too small. She should be at least 7 inches (17.78 centimeters) long.

2. Cut out your mermaid.

3. Look at your mermaid and decide where her tail begins. Ask a grown-up to begin cutting out the inside of your puppet's tail to create a frame for the tissue-paper scales.

4. Tear little bits of the tissue paper. Glue one side of each piece and place them inside the tail frame, building from the edges of the cut-out section. Cover the entire opening with the bits of torn tissue paper.

5. Using a pencil point or needle, poke two holes into the center of the mermaid.

6. Pull the paper clip slightly apart and push one end through the first hole from the back of the mermaid. Then push the same end back through the second hole. You should see only a loop on the front side of the puppet.

7. Tape the dowel to the paper clip on the back of the puppet to manipulate the puppet.

THE THEATER
What You Need
- Large cardboard box (microwave-oven size)
- Scissors
- Tissue paper or sheer fabric
- Tape or stapler
- Light source
- A grown-up to assist

What You Do
1. Ask a grown-up to cut out the bottom of the box. Cut off the flaps of the top of the box. Turn the box on one of its sides so it looks like a tunnel.

2. Cover one open end with the tissue paper or fabric to create your screen. Attach the screen to the box with the tape or stapler.

3. Place your theater box on a table with a light source (flashlight, window, or lamp) behind the box. The stronger the light source, the more clear your shadow puppets will appear.

4. Hold your puppet between the light source and the screen, keeping yourself out of the light source as much as possible. You are now ready for your show. Think about other shadow puppets that you could add to your show. You could easily make fish and seaweed shadow puppets now that you have created your mermaid. Think up a story that involves a lot of action so you can make your shadow puppets dance around. You'll put on a great show for your family and friends!

"They were six beautiful children; but the youngest was the prettiest of them all; her skin was as clear and delicate as a rose-leaf, and her eyes as blue as the deepest sea; but, like all the others, she had no feet, and her body ended in a fish's tail."

—from Hans Christian Andersen's *The Little Mermaid*

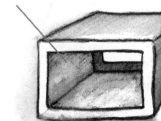

screen

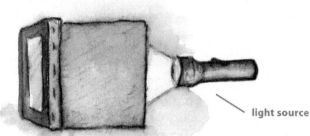

light source behind box

Sea Horses

If you have watched the movie *The Little Mermaid*, you have seen the wonderful sea horses that pull Ariel's father's chariot. These creatures might seem like something out of a fairy tale, but they are very real and very special.

There are four species of sea horses in North America. They make their home among sea grasses but also live among the submerged roots of mangrove trees, coral reefs, and estuaries (where rivers meet the sea). They range in size from 1 to 12 inches (2.54 to 30.48 centimeters). There are many special things about sea horses. For one, they can change their color to match their surroundings. That is, they *camouflage* themselves. This makes them difficult to see at times. They wrap their tails around blades of sea grass. Their bodies become the color of the grass, and they blend right in with the grasses.

Sea horses are also unique because they are *monogamous*. That means that they have only one mate, which is rare among fish. The most unusual thing about sea horses is that male sea horses are the ones that give birth to the babies, instead of the females. The female sea horse deposits fertilized eggs into the male's pouch, which is sort of like a kangaroo pouch. The eggs are protected in the pouch. Through capillaries in the pouch, the eggs receive oxygen and nutrients, just as babies do within an animal mother. When they are com-

pletely formed, they come out of the pouch and swim away.

Sassy Sea Horse Sculpture

Use polymer clay to create your own one-of-a-kind mythical sea horse, which can be made into a pin or to sit on a shelf.

What You Need

- Colored polymer clay (available at craft supply stores)
- Flat working surface
- Pencil
- Clay tools or toothpicks
- Glass beads and other decorative items
- Oven
- Pin back and glue (optional)
- A grown-up to assist

What You Do

1. Pick out the main color for your sea horse. This is a mythical sea horse so it can be any color you want.

2. If you want to create a flat sea horse that can be used as a pin, roll the clay into a ball and then flatten it out on your work surface. If you would like a sea horse that can sit on a shelf, also known as "in the round," then begin sculpting the body of your sea horse with the clay but don't flatten it.

3. If you're making a pin, you can outline the sea horse right on the flattened clay and then use the clay tools to remove the extra clay from around your design.

4. Lastly, decorate your pin or sculpture with glass beads, tiny multicolored clay dots, or any other ideas you have. Make it magical!

5. Ask a grown-up to bake your sea horse in an oven according to the directions on the package of the polymer clay. It will only take about 20 minutes to bake. When finished baking, let your sea horse cool completely.

6. Glue a pin back to your cooled sea horse or display your sculpture so that everyone can see it.

Dr. Amanda Vincent, Ocean Hero

Dr. Amanda Vincent's love of sea horses has led her to become the first scientist to have successfully studied them in their natural habitat. She began her study of sea horses more than 10 years ago, initially because she wanted to work with the sea and to be outdoors. As she began to work with sea horses, she became hooked. Through her research she learned that some sea horse populations had undergone a serious decline. She attributed this decline to the global trade in sea horses for aquariums, Chinese medicine, and souvenirs.

Dr. Vincent then took a different approach to her studies and began a crusade to save her sea horses. She set off for the Philippines to set up a sea horse conservation program. There, through the Haribon Founda-

tion, "grow-out cages" were built with the confiscated nets from illegal fishing. These grow-out cages are like corrals in the sea for the sea horses. Fishermen who catch young sea horses are paid three pesos, which comes to about 12 cents, for each young sea horse. The young sea horse is then placed in the "corral." It grows and has young. After about five months the fisherman is then allowed to sell the sea horse. The sea horse is larger and the fisherman is able to sell it for double its initial value. Meanwhile, the sea horse has been able to breed and increase the sea horse population. The newborn sea horses are able to escape through the nets of the grow-out cages and live in the wild. Sometimes a sea horse is captured that has young growing in its pouch. These sea horses are also put into the corral so that the young are able to survive. After the young are born, the male sea horse is then offered for sale.

Dr. Vincent has teamed up with the Zoological Society of London to form Project Sea Horse. Look in the resources section for information on how you can help Project Sea Horse.

What's Below?

Is there life below the shallow, sunlit waters? Of course! Let's take a dive and see what lurks in the dark depths of the ocean.

Dive into the Deep

5

Imagine you are in a submarine diving deep into the ocean. You look out the portholes and the sea around you becomes darker and darker. Soon you enter the twilight zone, 656 to 3,280 feet (199.95 to 999.74 meters) down, where fish glow and sea creatures seem too big to be real. It is a world where whales swim, a world that not many people see. Exploring this world of blue light and strange creatures is impossible without the help of a *submersible* that can take people safely into the ocean depths, but turn the page and you can enter into this most fascinating part of the ocean in the safety of your own room.

There Is Life Below

Early scientists believed that life could never exist in the dark ocean depths. In fact, Edward Forbes, a well-known British naturalist, claimed in 1843 that no animal could survive below about 1,800 feet (548.64 meters). He was proven wrong in the 1950s when the Galathea Expedition brought up sea cucumbers, sea anemones, a bristle worm, and other creatures from the depths of the Philippine Trench, the third-deepest trench of the ocean floor. At its deepest point, the depth of the trench measures 34,580 feet (10,540 meters).

In the last 50 years, oceanographers have discovered many previously unknown species of fish and sea creatures that are able to live in the deepest waters of the ocean.

The Darkest Dark

All wavelengths of light are absorbed at a depth of 800 feet (243.84 meters) below the ocean surface. This means that the deep water is the darkest blue-black you can imagine. How do you think the fish see other fish? How can they find food or a mate? Think about creatures that come out at night. How do they adapt to the darkness of the night? Some have big eyes, such as owls. Some use sound to find food, such as bats. All of these creatures feed and find mates when it's dark, but the dark of the night on land is nothing like the dark of the ocean because there are still stars and a moon to add light to the night. The creatures that live in the deepest parts of the ocean live where there is no light at all.

Glow-in-the-Dark Fish Picture

Fireflies, sometimes called lightning bugs, find each other at night by flashing a light on their body. The fish that live in and below the twilight zone use the same sort of body lights. The word that describes the light that these fish have is *bioluminescence*. The fish have a substance called luciferin. A chemical reaction occurs between an enzyme called luciferase, oxygen, and the luciferin. As a result, energy is released in the form of light.

Taillights, headlights, and rows of beacon lights illuminate the fish. Most of this bioluminescence is blue-green. Creatures that are closely related have minor differences in arrangements and sizes of these lights. For example, one species of lantern fish has three rows of lights, while another has two. These differences help the fish to recognize each other and form schools.

You may not be able to dive into the deep ocean depths to see these creatures firsthand, but here's a way that you can create your own glowing fish. You may even want to create a whole school of them when you finish!

What You Need
→ Black or dark blue construction paper
→ Pencil
→ Glow-in-the-dark paint (available at craft supply stores)
→ Toothpicks

What You Do
1. Pretend your construction paper is the deepest part of the ocean, where fish use light to find food and friends.
2. Using your pencil, lightly draw some fish on your paper.
3. Dip your toothpick into the glow-in-the-dark paint. Lightly dab the paint onto the fish in different patterns. Remember, some fish have rows of lights, some have headlights, and others have lights on their tails.
4. Turn off the lights and watch your fish glow! Your finished picture probably looks very much like it does way below the ocean surface.

Flashlight Fish

The flashlight fish is aptly named because it has large light organs right below its eyes that contain *luminous*, a glowing bacteria. These lights make it easy for the flashlight fish to see in the dark waters; however, these lights also make it easy for predators to see them. How do they hide from their enemies? Easy, they switch off their lights.

Home of the Giants

Most of the fish that live in the deep are small, but the invertebrates (creatures without backbones, such as sea urchins, shrimp, squid, and others) grow to be much larger than their shallow-water relatives. For example, shallow-water sea urchins and shrimp grow to a few inches or so, compared to their deep-water counterparts that reach a foot (30.48 centimeters) in size. Sea pens, which resemble old-fashioned quill pens, grow to about two feet (60.96 centimeters) in shallow water but can reach lengths of eight feet (243.84 centimeters) in deep water.

Squid, on the other hand, have a gargantuan relative living deep in the ocean—the giant squid. To imagine a giant squid, try the next couple of activities.

Examine a Squid

Put on your scientist gear and examine the common squid. Then, in the next activity, you can think a lot bigger and imagine what a giant squid looks like.

What You Need
- A squid, preferably not cleaned
- Cutting board or other flat surface
- Ruler

What You Do

1. Visit a seafood market and ask the salesperson if he or she has any whole squid. You will most likely find cleaned squid pieces in one of the cases, but you want to look at a squid that has not been cleaned and cut up yet.

2. When you get home, unwrap your squid and examine it with your hands. How does it feel? Is it smooth? How many tentacles does it have? Is it heavy or light for its size? What do you think it weighs?

3. Place your squid on a cutting board or other flat surface. Can you find the squid's beak? It resembles a bird's beak and is used for eating. How about the mantle? The mantle is the long tube that makes up the body of the squid.

4. Measure your squid with a ruler. How long is it? How long are the tentacles?

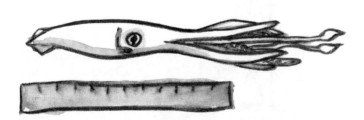

_____ centimeters?

Giant Squid Size Study

A giant squid can grow to more than 60 feet (18.29 meters) in length! Let's see how long that is.

What You Need

➤ Tape measure
➤ Several friends
➤ Paper
➤ Pencil

What You Do

1. Ask a friend or grown-up to measure your length. How many inches (centimeters) tall are you? How many inches taller are you than the common squid you measured in the previous activity?

2. Measure each of your friends. Write down their measurements so that you can remember them.

3. Think about a squid that is 60 feet (18.29 meters) long. If you laid down each of your friends and yourself in a long line from head to toe, how long would your line be? Use the tape measure to find out. How many friends do you have to add or subtract to the line to reach 60 feet (18.29 meters)?

4. Look at the little squid that you measured in the previous activity. Can you now imagine a squid that is 60 feet long?

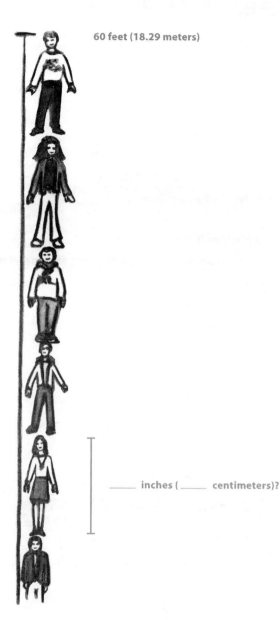

60 feet (18.29 meters)

_____ inches (_____ centimeters)?

More About Squid and Octopuses

Where in the World Are Giant Squid?

Giant squid have long been a mystery to scientists because they have not been able to study healthy, living examples in the wild. Almost everything we know about these large creatures we have learned from studying giant squid that have been found dead or near death by fishermen who have found them floating in the water. Where are these huge creatures found and why haven't we seen them? Well, most of the squid have been found in the waters of Norway, New Zealand, and Newfoundland. It is believed that they live between 650 to 2,000 feet (198.12 m to 609.6 meters) below the ocean surface but probably swim even deeper.

Kraken

There have been stories dating back to the 12th century in Norway about a sea monster called the *kraken*. These stories described the kraken as a huge creature with many arms and as big as an island. The kraken was so large that ships needed to look out for this monster, because it could wrap its arms around the ship and capsize it. We now think that the large animals that the sailors reported off the coast of Norway were giant squid. The giant squid were larger than the sailing ships of those times and could very well have frightened a sailor. Although there have never been recorded cases of giant squid capsizing a ship, it is likely that a giant squid could mistake a ship for an enemy sperm whale and possibly attack the ship.

Real Blue Bloods

Squid and octopuses belong to the class Cephalopoda of mollusks. These invertebrates have three hearts, two that help the gills and one that actually pumps blue blood! The hemoglobin that makes our blood red is absent from squid and octopuses. Instead, these creatures have hemocyanin, which is a blue blood pigment. But don't expect to see bright blue blood when you examine a squid. It actually looks more clear than blue.

Ocean Notion

If you have eaten in an Italian or seafood restaurant, you have probably seen calamari on the menu. *Calamari* is squid. The word *calamari* comes from the Medieval Latin word *calamarium*, which means "ink pot." Squid and octopuses all produce ink. Like a superhero that is able to release a smoke field to escape an enemy, these creatures can release ink into the water around them. The ink surrounds and confuses the approaching enemy, allowing the squid or octopus time to escape.

Quick-Change Artists

Have you ever seen a chameleon change color? It's fun to pick up a chameleon and place it on something green and then watch it turn green. Well, squid and octopuses can also change color, even quicker than a chameleon. In an instant they can change their skin color to match their surroundings. An octopus can also change the texture of its skin. This is the ultimate form of camouflage. Can you imagine having the ability to change color and texture?

The Mimic Octopus

The mimic octopus is one of the most amazing octopuses. Not only can it change color and texture, but it can actually make its body resemble some dangerous ocean creatures, such as the lionfish, the sea anemone, and a black-and-white-striped sea snake. Found in the waters around Indonesia, this octopus adopts the coloration and shape of these creatures. Since octopuses have no bones, they have tremendous flexibility with their bodies. They can hide in a small hole and poke their arms up out of the hole to look like an anemone. What better way to keep predators away?

The Octopus Garden

There's a Beatles song by Ringo Starr aptly titled "Octopus's Garden." Listen to it when you have the chance. The octopus is one of the few marine creatures, perhaps the only one, that actually creates its own little garden outside its home by placing empty shells—the remains of its meals—around the entrance to its cave.

Octopus Periscope

Octopuses have the ability to move one eye in one direction and the other eye in another direction at the same time. They can also move their eyes almost all the way around. Some octopuses can even raise their eyes like a periscope. Here's a periscope you can make to examine the world above the waves.

What You Need

- 2 1-quart (or 1-liter) milk cartons
- Scissors
- 2 small, flat mirrors
- Masking tape
- A grown-up to assist

What You Do

1. Use the scissors to cut off the peaked tops of the milk cartons.

2. Cut a hole about 3 inches (7.62 centimeters) in diameter at the bottom of each milk carton on one side.

3. Place a mirror inside each milk carton, tilted with the shiny side of the mirror facing the hole that you cut in the side. Tape the mirror in place.

4. Tape the two cartons together so that one hole is on the bottom right side and one hole is on the top left side.

5. Take a look through the bottom hole in your periscope to see over things that are taller than you. Hold it sideways to peer around corners.

cut off tops

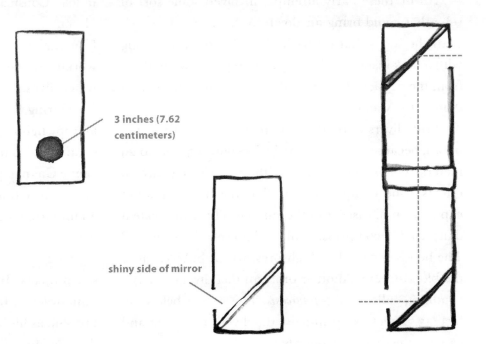

3 inches (7.62 centimeters)

shiny side of mirror

Then and Now

What would you use to explore the ocean? A submarine? A submersible? Diving gear? Thankfully, today there are choices, but this was not always the case. In earlier times scientists had questions, such as how deep is the ocean, and did not have the equipment to answer them. There were many attempts to develop a safe way to travel beneath the ocean surface. In fact, even Leonardo da Vinci tried his hand at designing a diving machine. These early attempts led to underwater suits of armor and chambers that would carry a person below the waves.

All of these early attempts involved some sort of tube that could bring air down to the divers. It wasn't until the 1950s that divers had the freedom of diving with a tank instead of having air pumped down to them from the surface. This gave the divers much more freedom in the water.

Still, divers were unable to reach many parts of the ocean, because divers can safely dive only 165 feet (50.29 meters) below the surface without suffering any ill effects. The compressed air that the diver breathes expands on his ascent to the surface. This can create a dangerous decompression illness known as "the bends." The bends occur when high-pressure air bubbles enter the bloodstream. Another problem that divers face is a condition called *nitrogen narcosis*. This occurs below 150 feet (45.72 meters). It impairs the diver's judgment and can put the diver in jeopardy.

Divers still wanted to reach the greater ocean depths, which are as far as seven miles (11.27 kilometers) below the ocean surface in some areas. Only a submersible released from a submarine can successfully travel to these great depths. A small remote camera on a submersible can open up unseen worlds to us.

Jacques Cousteau, Ocean Hero

Jacques Cousteau was a true ocean hero. Born in France in 1910, Cousteau never had the ocean far from his mind. He entered the Naval Academy upon his graduation from high school. There he began exploring the sea and working on developing a breathing machine for underwater dives.

During World War II Jacques Cousteau spent time as a spy fighting for the French. All the while, Cousteau continued his undersea work. In 1943, he and engineer Emile Gagnan perfected the Aqua Lung, which allowed divers more time underwater. The Aqua Lung was also an important contribution to the war effort. It was later used to locate and disarm underwater mines.

Cousteau finally left the navy to pursue more undersea projects. In 1950 he purchased a converted U.S. minesweeper. It was christened *Calypso*. Cousteau used this ship as his base for many years. From it he produced documentary films and many books about the sea. In

1968 he introduced millions of people to the undersea world he loved through a television series that continued for eight years. The episodes of *The Undersea World of Jacques Cousteau* focused on sunken treasure, sharks, dolphins, coral reefs, and much more.

Cousteau, who died at age 87 in 1997, proved to be an invaluable conservationist and protector of the world's oceans throughout his life. The Cousteau Society, formed in 1974 by Jacques Cousteau, still conducts ocean research and promotes education of the undersea world.

the other end, a red plume, waved about in the water. These giant tube worms were found to grow up to four feet (1.22 meters) tall and to feed on bacteria. But the most amazing thing about these worms was that they were found to grow 33 inches (83.82 centimeters) each year, which makes them the fastest-growing marine invertebrate. If you grew 33 inches this year, how tall would you be?

Discoveries on the Ocean Floor

In 1977 a three-person submersible named *Alvin* enabled scientists to make an important discovery in the waters off the Galapagos Islands. More than 8,000 feet (2,438.4 meters) below the ocean surface they found hot thermal vents, like underwater geysers, spouting hot acidic water. The vents were generally about a half inch (1.27 centimeters) to about six feet (1.83 meters) in diameter. The discovery of these hot thermal vents has led scientists to identify over 300 new marine species, including many different marine worms. Near the vents were clusters of giant tube worms, a species previously unknown to scientists. The worms were found with one end of the worm, a white tube, anchored to the ocean floor, while

Window on the Undersea World

What do you think you would see from the porthole of a submersible as you traveled down into the depths of the sea? Perhaps you would see a lot of seaweed, colorful fish, and a sea turtle. Maybe you traveled further down into the depths and could see flashlight fish and giant tube worms. You can create your very own window from your imaginary submersible.

What You Need

- 2 paper plates
- Scissors
- Blue plastic wrap
- White craft glue
- Construction paper
- Pencil
- Glitter and other decorative items
- Stapler

What You Do

1. Use the scissors to cut out the center of each paper plate to create the frame for your window, or porthole.

2. Glue the plastic wrap to the inside frame of each paper plate.

3. Now it's time to create the creatures you see from your window. Draw your sea creatures on the construction paper. Cut them out and decorate them however you like.

4. Glue the sea creatures to the inside frames of the paper plates so that they hang down into the center of the plates that are covered with plastic wrap. You might want to leave a few of the creatures free to float inside the window.

5. Place the two paper plates together so that the creatures and plastic wrap face each other. Staple or glue the two plates together. Now take a look through your window and imagine you are sailing through the water in a submersible.

Something's Missing

All this talk of oceans and no real fish yet? Turn the page for a very fishy tale!

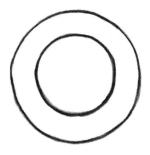
Cut out center.

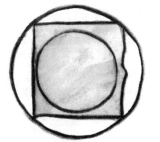
plastic wrap

Staple plates together.

6

Gone Fishing

There are at least 20,000 different kinds of fish in the ocean. If there are that many different *kinds* of ocean fish, can you imagine how many *total* fish there are in the ocean? It's an enormous number. Even so, that doesn't mean that we can take all these fish for granted. We rely on them for many things, mainly food. The health of our ocean is important to the fish populations. We need to take care of the ocean and its fish so that we can make sure that future generations will be able to enjoy them. Now, let's throw out a line and see what we can discover when we reel it in!

What Makes a Fish a Fish?

All fish have certain things in common. They are all *vertebrate* animals, which means they have a backbone, fins, and internal gills. There are three classes of fish—primitive jawless fish, sharklike fish, and bony fish. Most fish are cold-blooded, which means they are unable to self-regulate their body temperature and need to rely on their environment for their temperature. Fish are found in all kinds of water and, as we know now, at all depths of water. Some fish are *carnivorous*, or meat-eating. Others are *herbivorous*, or plant-eating. Still others are *omnivorous*, which means they eat both plants and animals.

Wild-About-Oceans T-Shirt

Gyotaku (pronounced ghio-ta´-koo) is the Japanese art of fish printing. It has been used for centuries to record fish that were caught. It involves spreading paint on the fish and then pressing a piece of rice paper over the inked

Ocean Notion
Fish have backbones, just like us. Fish breath oxygen, just like us. A fish releases carbon dioxide, just like us. Fish have scales that are platelike and the same structure as our fingernails. In what ways are fish different from us?

fish. This activity is inspired by this ancient art form, but instead of using real fish, you can create your own. You can use your fish to make prints on paper or to show off your ocean pride with this fishy T-shirt.

What You Need
- 1 white T-shirt, washed and dried
- Cardboard
- Kitchen sponges
- Pencil
- Scissors
- Water
- Fabric paint (available at craft supply stores)
- Fabric paint marker (available at craft supply stores)

What You Do
1. Wash and dry your T-shirt without using any fabric softener that would hinder the paint from adhering to the fabric. Place a sheet of cardboard inside the shirt so that the paint does not seep through to the back of the shirt.
2. Use the pencil to draw fish shapes on your sponges and then cut them out. Soften up your sponges with a little water to make them a bit easier to sponge-paint with.
3. Dip the fish shapes into your fabric paint. Make sure you have an even coverage of paint on the sponge.
4. Press the fish shape onto the T-shirt. Create your fish design using the different shapes of fish.
5. Complete your T-shirt by writing "I AM WILD ABOUT OCEANS" or another saying on your shirt with the fabric marker. You might even want to put your school name on it

and have a fish represent each of your classmates. Remember, fish swim in schools!

cardboard

I Am Wild About Oceans

sponge

Another Fishy Idea

Make a bunch of tiny little fish by using your very own thumbprint. Dip your thumb in the paint and press it onto the T-shirt. Draw fins and a tail on your tiny fish with the fabric marker.

Flat Fish

Picture a fish in your mind. What does it look like? It probably has a football or torpedolike shape, fins and eyes on each side, a tail, and a mouth right in the front. Well, that does fit the description of a lot of fish, but there are others, such as flounder, that look a bit different. A flounder is flat, but it doesn't start out that way. When it is born it looks very much like other fish. After a few days, however, it starts to lean to one side. The eye that is on that side starts to move over to the other side. Weird, huh? Pretty soon the founder is flat and both eyes are on the top. It then swims down to the ocean floor where it lives as an adult fish.

Why the Flounder Is Flat and Has Two Eyes on One Side

Here's a version of a folktale from Polynesia that tries to explain the flatness of the flounder.

There were once a lobster and a flounder that liked to play hide-and-seek. The problem was that the lobster's antennae would always give it away. The flounder would look for the lobster and find the antennae sticking up from behind a rock or coral. This made the lobster very upset. To make matters worse, the lobster always had a very hard time finding the flounder. This happened again and again. One day the lobster got very angry.

When the flounder finally came out of his hiding place, the lobster rushed over and stamped on the flounder until he was flat. With all that stamping, the poor flounder's eye fell into the sand. The lobster felt bad for what he had done and picked up the flounder's eye and placed it next to the other one. That is why the flounder is still flat and why he has two eyes on the same side.

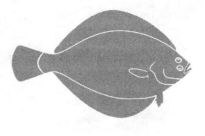

When Is a Fish Not a Fish?

There are many creatures in the sea that are called fish that aren't true fish, such as starfish and jellyfish. There are other sea creatures that people commonly mistake for fish, but are also not true fish, such as dolphins, which are really mammals. Can you think of other sea creatures that are mistaken for fish? How about thinking of sea creatures that are really fish but aren't thought of as fish, such as a sea horse? Remember, a true fish has fins, gills, and a backbone.

Creature Feature: Devilfish or Friendly Giants?

There are more than 400 species of rays in the ocean. These species are divided into seven families: stingrays, skates, manta rays, guitarfish, electric rays, and eagle rays. All are fish and are relatives of sharks. Just like sharks they have skeletons of cartilage instead of bone. Some rays are armed against their predators with poisonous spines and whiplike tails, which makes some people call them "devilfish." But not all rays are dangerous. In fact, the huge manta rays that can grow to be 20 feet (6.09 meters) wide and weigh over 3,500 pounds (1,587.57 kilograms) are harmless to humans. They feed on small fish and plankton, which they filter from the water. Their wings ripple and flutter as they "fly" through the water.

The Ray That Eats Like a Cow

Well, of course it eats like a cow—it's a cownose ray! The cownose ray is found from the waters of Brazil to the waters of Massachusetts. And it does indeed eat like a cow! It flaps its wings to churn up the ocean bottom and uncover oysters, clams, and other tasty bivalves. In fact, the rays have really taken a bite out of the Chesapeake Bay shellfish populations.

Why Don't Fish Drown?

Fish need air to breathe and yet they don't drown in the water. How come? Well, fish don't breathe air, as we do. Instead, fish take in oxygen from the water. Fish have gills that act like our lungs. The water passes into their mouths and over their gills. The blood vessels in the gills absorb the oxygen in the water. Carbon dioxide is then released from the gills into the ocean water.

Ocean Racers

Our Olympic swimmers can't hold a candle to some fish swimming in the open ocean waters. These fish are designed to swim fast. Their bodies are sleek and slippery. In fact, sailfish, swordfish, and some tuna have been clocked swimming in bursts up to almost 70 miles (112.65 kilometers) per hour.

Ocean Notion
Take a look at a bottle of sparkling water or club soda. Can you see that gas is dissolved in the water? In a similar way, oxygen is dissolved in the water of the ocean.

Mexican Fish Yarn Painting

Mexican yarn paintings are fun to create. Many yarn paintings depict animals or flowers. The original designs were much simpler than they are today. Take a look in the resources section for links to yarn paintings on the Web. They will inspire your own creations.

What You Need
- Oak tag or cardboard
- Crayons or markers
- White craft glue
- Yarn or embroidery floss of various colors, cut in 6-inch (15.24 centimeters) lengths

What You Do
1. Draw a circle in the middle of your piece of oak tag. In the middle of the circle draw the outline of a fish.
2. Draw other fish, ocean creatures, seaweed, and shapes in the area outside of the circle.
3. Spread glue on the body of the fish drawing in the center of the circle.
4. Place pieces of yarn on the outside line of the fish body. Then fill in the body with the yarn strands. Cover the tail in the same way.
5. Next, spread glue around the fish inside the circle. Spread glue on all the surrounding space inside the circle. Working out from the fish, cover the entire circle in yarn.
6. Next, work on the shapes outside of the circle. Spread glue on each shape, then cover each shape with yarn.
7. To complete your picture, work on the space in between each of the shapes until all of the space is covered with yarn.

Fish Facts

Here are some fun fish facts that will fascinate your friends.

Smallest ocean fish: dwarf goby (less than a half inch [1.27 centimeters] long)

Largest ocean fish: whale shark (over 50 feet [15.24 meters] long)

Most common ocean fish: cyclothome, commonly known as the bristle-mouth fish

Fastest fish: sailfish (swims 68 miles [109.44 kilometers] per hour)

Slowest fish: sea horse (swims less than .001 miles [.0016 kilometers] per hour)

Most poisonous fish: pufferfish (a piece just the size of a quarter, about a quarter ounce, has enough poison to incapacitate a man in 10 to 20 minutes)

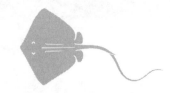

Pufferfish Piñata

How would you like to bite into something that could kill you if it wasn't prepared correctly? That's what many Japanese do when they bite into a delicacy known as *fugu*. *Fugu* is pufferfish. There are about 120 species of pufferfish, all of which can inflate their body with air or water to make themselves look like a balloon. Many pufferfish species have spines that stick out when they are inflated. But it is not the spines that are dangerous to diners; it is the poisonous flesh of the fish. Yet despite its danger, many people pay up to $400 for one meal. It takes a chef 3 years to learn how to prepare fugu and 15 years before the chef can open his or her own restaurant. Although most meals are prepared carefully, there are still approximately 50 deaths attributed to fugu poisoning each year in Japan.

Take the danger out of the pufferfish with this piñata filled with candy and sweets. Celebrate with an ocean party!

What You Need
- Flat working surface
- Newspaper
- Balloon
- Plastic bowl
- White craft glue
- Water
- Spoon
- Paint
- Paintbrush
- Pin
- Candy
- Small drill
- Wire or string
- Blindfold
- Broom
- A grown-up to assist

What You Do
1. Prepare your work area by covering it with newspaper.
2. Begin the project by tearing off long strips of newspaper, blowing up the balloon, and mixing the white craft glue in the bowl with some water to make a thin paste. Try a mixture of half glue and half water to make the paste.

3. Dip each strip of newspaper completely into the paste and place it on the balloon. Continue this process until you have covered the entire balloon except for a small hole on the bottom. Add two more layers.

4. Let the newspaper dry overnight on your piñata.

5. At this point your piñata looks like a ball, but here's how you make it look like a spiny pufferfish. Tear the newspaper strips into smaller squares. Dip each square into the paste. Roll the small squares into cones and press them onto the piñata. These will be the spines for your pufferfish.

6. Shape a tail with the newspaper and glue it onto the piñata at the opposite end of the hole.

7. Allow the piñata to dry completely and then paint it.

8. When the paint has completely dried, pop the balloon with a pin and fill the piñata with candy. Plug the hole with a few crumpled sheets of newspaper.

9. Complete the pufferfish by rolling up some of the newspaper to form two lips. Glue the lips where the hole used to be. When the lips are dry, paint them.

10. Have a grown-up drill a couple of holes in the top of your piñata. Thread a wire or string through the holes and hang your piñata. You're all set for your party! Have your friends line up and, one at a time, while blindfolded, take a swing at the pufferfish with a broom to try and break the piñata and release the candy.

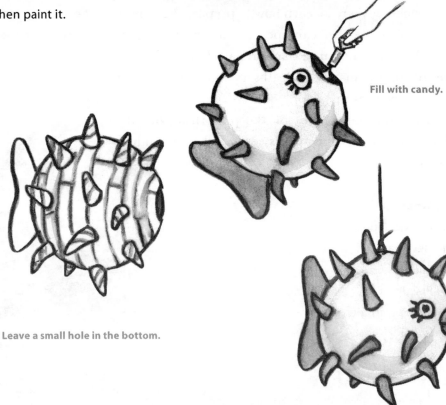

strips of newspaper

Leave a small hole in the bottom.

Fill with candy.

The Sixth Sense

We have five different senses. We have the sense of taste, smell, and touch. We can also see and hear. Fish have these same senses, but they also have another: the *lateral line*. The *lateral line* is a system of sensory receptors that form a canal along the head and sides of the fish. Pores on the fish's skin allow water to carry sound vibrations into the lateral line, where the lateral nerve carries the messages to the brain of the fish. The fish is able to detect movements and pressure changes in the water around it. In this way, the fish can tell if another fish is swimming nearby or if there is a disturbance in the water.

If you had a sixth sense, what would you like it to be?

The One That May Get Away

We are so used to seeing seafood on restaurant menus that we couldn't imagine that any of these fish could be endangered. After all, we already know that there are 20,000 species of fish in the ocean and the ocean is huge, so how can there be any shortage?

Unfortunately, many fish species *are* in danger. Our technology has increased so dramatically in the fishing industry that many fish don't have a chance against it. There are now spotter planes and modern fishing boats

Ocean Notion

It is smart to stay in school. Fish stay in schools, too. They group together in schools for protection and mating. The school also helps them swim better, because all the fish in the school are moving through the water at the same time in the same direction.

that easily locate fish. In addition, the new fishing methods are nonselective, which means that they catch a lot of other creatures, such as sea turtles, diving birds, young fish, and dolphins, not just the particular type of fish they're after. This side effect of modern fishing is called bycatch. The *bycatch*, or other species caught but not wanted, usually end up being killed in the process. In fact, in 1994 the United Nations reported that for every pound of shrimp caught in the Sea of Cortez, nearly 10 pounds of other marine life died in the bycatch before released into the water.

Let's review some of these fishing methods. One is the *longline*, which is a long cable held in place with buoys, with as many as 3,000 baited hooks attached to the line. Any fish or marine animal that tries to eat the bait may become hooked. It has been reported that these longlines killed 500,000 marlin and 150,000 sailfish in 1996. The targeted fish for the longlines were swordfish and tuna.

What about the swordfish? Did they catch a lot of swordfish as well as the marlin and sailfish? The swordfish population has dwindled considerably to the point that it might disappear from our future menus. Many restaurant chefs recognize the plight of the swordfish and have taken the fish off of their menus in an effort to help increase this fish population. The Give Swordfish a Break campaign was a good start, but more action is needed.

Ocean Fish Action List

Here are a few things you can do to conserve ocean fish populations.

1. Look for seafood with Marine Stewardship certification. This label is a white fish on a blue background. This label indicates that strict guidelines have been followed to ensure the conservation of fish populations.

2. Avoid buying or eating the top ocean predators, such as shark, tuna, and swordfish. These species of fish have suffered depleted populations because as the top fish of the food chain, there are less of them to go around. Instead, choose lower food-chain fish that are more abundant, such as squid.

3. Avoid caviar altogether. The population of sturgeon is greatly in danger.

4. Learn more about dredging, trawling, and other modern fishing methods from the glossary below. Talk about which ones might damage the ocean habitat and which ones might not.

5. Go into your local fish stores and ask them about their fish. Find out if their salmon are farm raised, if their clams are gathered by dredging the ocean floor, or if their shrimp are harvested by trawling. All of these practices are ecologically damaging to the fish and the environment.

6. Write letters to supermarket chains and tell them that you are concerned about the fish they carry. Tell them about some fishing methods that are damaging to the ocean. Offer them some better alternatives, such as wild salmon instead of farm-raised salmon. Write about certain species that are overfished.

Glossary of Terms Related to Modern Fishing Methods

Bycatch: The ocean wildlife that is caught along with the species of fish that is desired.

Dredging: Scraping the ocean floor to harvest clams, mussels, and other shellfish.

Harvesting machine: A machine that uses a pump with a light to attract fish and squid and then sucks them up onto the deck of the boat. Unfortunately, this can easily damage the catch. Only small fish can be harvested without injury.

Longlining: Extending a long cable into the ocean with many, many baited hooks.

Overfished: A situation that occurs when a species of fish has been fished so much that its population is depleted significantly.

Trawling: Catching fish using a cone-shaped net that is dragged through the water or along the bottom of the ocean.

Fishing Fun

Some modern fishing practices are damaging to the ocean, but the tried-and-true method of casting a line into the ocean is still a great way to catch fish. After you catch one, you can even toss it back. This is called *catch-and-release fishing*. Here's how to start.

What You Need
- Bait
- Hooks
- Fishing rod and reel
- Fishing line
- Weights
- A grown-up to assist

What You Do

1. Find out the fishing regulations in your area. Kids don't usually need any license to fish, but if the grown-up with you wants to fish, he or she must get a license.

2. Find a spot to fish. It's fun to fish right off the shore. This is called *shore angling*. You can also fish from a dock or a boat. Make sure to wear a life preserver if you are fishing on a dock or a boat.

3. You'll need to buy the right bait for the fish that are in your area. A good bait shop will help you select the right bait.

4. Have a grown-up flatten the sharp little barbs that stick out of your hooks so that you can easily release any fish you catch.

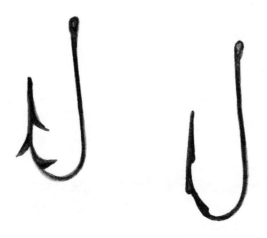

5. Have a grown-up prepare your rod and reel with fishing line, weights, and hook.

6. Now you are ready to fish. Have a grown-up bait your hook. If you are on a dock or a boat, you just need to drop your line into the water. If you are fishing from shore, you need to cast your line beyond the waves. Ask a grown-up to show you how to cast the first few times.

7. Reel a little line in until you feel a little bit of pull on your line. This way it will be easy to feel if a fish bites your bait.

8. If you feel a fish take your bait, begin reeling your line in slowly. If you pull too fast, you might lose your fish.

9. Have the grown-up take your catch off your hook and toss the fish back into the water.

Moving On

Let's step back for a moment and search out some of the other creatures that inhabit the ocean. You might even find some of them out of the ocean and on the beach!

Search for Shells, Sand, and Surprises

Have you ever received a gift of a seashell or found one on a beach? If you have, then you are lucky. Seashells are beautiful. They have been worn as jewelry, been inspiration for architects, and even served as money. Poets proclaim their beauty. More importantly, seashells are the homes of many soft, invertebrate animals. These animals, called *mollusks*, create these shells that we love. As the animal grows, it slowly adds a liquid substance to the edge of its shell to increase the size of the shell. It also has special glands that add color to the shell before the new layers become hard.

Walk along a beach and you might find evidence of these creatures. It might be a beautiful, whole shell that you find, but often it might just be a piece of one. What else can you find on the beach? Every beach is different. Some have mounds and drifts of white sand, while others might be covered with smooth, round stones. Still other beaches have bits of smooth glass polished by years of ocean tumbling.

Come and explore the wonderful edge of the ocean and see what you can discover on the shore.

calico scallop

Amazing Mollusks

There are many creatures that live in shells in the ocean. They are called mollusks.

Just like snails that you find in a garden, sea snails have a shell. There are many different species of sea snails. They are all known as *univalves*, meaning they have one shell. Whelks, conchs, top shells, moon snails, nutmegs, and periwinkles are all different types of sea snails. Univalve mollusks have a trap door, called an *operculum*. You can see the operculum when you pick up a live shell. The mollusk living inside the shell will close the trap door to protect itself. You can see the smooth, hard operculum closing off the opening of the shell.

Bivalves are mollusks that have a two-part, hinged shell. Clams, mussels, oysters, cockles, and scallops are all bivalves. Mollusks that live in a hinged shell do not have an operculum. Instead, these creatures just hold their two shells tightly together to close off their opening.

When you find a shell at the beach, carefully look inside to see if the animal is alive or if the animal has died and left the shell empty. If the animal is still alive, you can watch it for a while before placing it back where you found it.

The Crawling Gastropods

Sea snails belong to the class of mollusks known as *gastropods*. There are more than 60,000 species of gastropods in the world. The word *gastropod* comes from two Greek words, *gaster* meaning "stomach" and *podos* meaning "foot." Most gastropods have a large foot that enables them to crawl around the ocean floor. This foot also helps certain species to burrow into the sand and swim.

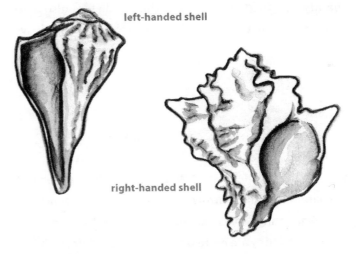

whelk shell

Left- or Right-Handed

Did you know that shells can be right- or left-handed? Find out which shells are right-handed and which ones are left-handed with this simple exercise.

What You Need
➤ Univalve shells (whelks, periwinkles, snails, and so on)

What You Do
1. Hold the shell in your left hand with its pointed tail, called the *channel*, pointing toward you and its pointed top, or *spire*, pointing away from you. The opening should be facing up.

2. What side is the opening on? If the opening is on the right side and you can place your right hand into the opening without crossing over the shell, then the shell is considered right-handed. If you have to switch hands to place your left hand in the opening without crossing over, then it is considered a left-handed shell.

left-handed shell

right-handed shell

Except for lightning whelks, which are mostly left-handed shells, a left-handed shell is difficult to find.

The Sound of the Sea

Hold a seashell up to your ear. Can you hear the sound of the ocean? Some say that the sound you hear is caused by the noise of your blood rushing through the arteries in your ear. Others say that slight breezes and faint background noises cause the air to resonate. This means that the shell acts like the sound box of a guitar or violin and magnifies this faint background noise.

Shell Board

Visit any seashore resort area and you're bound to see seashell display boards at shops and motels. They are a handy way to identify your findings. They're also a great way to display your own shells. Here's how to make your own.

What You Need
- Wooden board or shingle (any size)
- Shells
- Tacky glue (available at craft supply stores)
- Markers

What You Do

1. Wash all the shells that you are planning to use for your board. Rinse them and dry them.

2. Begin laying out your shells on your board, deciding where you want to place each shell. Be sure to leave room to label each shell.

3. Pick up each shell, dip it in tacky glue, and place it back on the board in the same place.

4. Once the shells are completely dry, use your marker to label each shell. Write the shell name directly on the board. A shell reference guide will help you find the names of your shells. This is also a great way to display rock collections.

Ocean Notion

Many people have written about shells. The poet Robert Louis Stevenson once said, "It is perhaps a fortunate destiny to have a taste for collecting shells than to be born a millionaire." What do you think he meant? Do you agree? Writer and naturalist Anne Morrow Lindbergh wrote in her famous book, *Gift from the Sea*, "One cannot collect all the beautiful shells on the beach. One can collect only a few, and they are more beautiful if they are few." Think about what she wrote. What would make you happier: a few special shells or a whole bucketful?

Hitching a Ride

Did you ever pick up a shell that had other shells attached to it? Often live shells, such as slipper shells, attach to a larger shell, such as a tulip shell. They live upon the other shell without causing any damage to it. Some shells, called *carrier shells*, actually pick up other shells. Sometimes the shells that they pick up are the shells of dead bivalves. The carrier shell actually secretes a gluelike substance that sticks the other shells onto its own shell. What do you think is the purpose for collecting all of these other shells? Scientists are not quite sure but think that it might make it harder for the shell to be eaten by fish. Some other scientists think that it prevents the animal from sinking into the mud of the ocean. Come up with your own idea. There are 20 known species of carrier shells in the world.

Window to the Past

There are so many areas of the world that were once covered by ocean. Today, ancient shells are found in many of these areas. In Florida, fossil shells ranging from 100,000 to 50 million years old have been found throughout the state. These shells are different from other fossils in that they are not mineralized, meaning that their original material has not been replaced. In the case of fossilized plants, the plants are no longer there.

Fossil shells are actual shells of that age. Finding one of these fossilized shells is not always difficult. Open mining pits near Sarasota, Florida, and other areas are often accessible to the public. Shells that are not collected from these pits by collectors are used for road and parking lot fill.

These pits are not the only places to find these shells. They can also be found on beaches and other places where ancient rivers carried material. It's fun to look at these fossil shells and compare them to the modern shells that are found today. Some do not have a modern counterpart, but many do and changes can be seen between them.

Ocean Notion

What do a whelk and an elephant have in common? Whelks have a feeding tube called a *proboscis*. The proboscis acts very much like an elephant's trunk in gathering food.

Make Your Own Shell Fossils

Fossil shells are not the only type of fossils that collectors may find. Fossils are also formed by the imprints of shells in mud or some other material and are called *trace fossils*. After millions of years, these imprints remain. Here's a way for you to make your own trace fossils, and you don't have to wait very long to see your results.

What You Need

➡ Shells—scallops work great (available at craft supply stores or fish markets)

➡ Petroleum jelly

➡ Air-drying clay (available at craft supply stores)

What You Do

1. Rub the petroleum jelly over the surface of a clean, dry shell. This will keep the shell from sticking to the clay.

2. Push the shell down into the clay. Make sure that the clay makes contact with the whole surface.

3. Gently pry the shell out of the clay and take a look at your imprint. If you are not happy with it, reform the clay and try again. You can make multiple imprints in the clay.

4. Let the clay dry. You can use the completed fossil for a paperweight.

Push shell into clay.

Money Challenge

In 1924, if you wanted to buy a pig in the New Guinea highlands, all you needed were five cowrie shells. In fact the word *cowrie* comes from a Greek word that means "little pig." Pigs weren't the only thing that you could buy with a stash of cowrie shells, however. You could buy anything. Perhaps your family wanted a chicken, or gold; if you had enough cowrie shells, you could buy whatever you needed.

Cowrie shells, specifically the money cowrie, were the most widely and longest-used currency in our history. They were found in tombs in ancient Egypt and China. In fact, they were used as recently as the middle of the 20th century in parts of Africa.

The little shell is found in the Indo-Pacific Ocean region. It is shaped like a dome with a cleft on the bottom. It looks like a circle that has been folded on either side, forming a rounded top and a fold on the bottom. The Greeks thought that it resembled the back of a pig.

Other shells have also been used as money. Native Americans used parts of whelks and tusk shells as money. On the Solomon Islands, where cowries were abundant, islanders carved round disks from clam shells to use as money.

Pretend you are the chief of your own island. You need to set up your own currency to trade with other islands. Let's explore how to go about doing this.

What You Need

➤ Stones, seeds, shells, or other objects

What You Do

1. Think about the objects that you want to trade as currency. How would you determine their value? Have you ever traded baseball or Pokemon cards with your friends? What makes certain cards more valuable? Could you trade a card for something else that you wanted?

2. Where would you get your currency? Does it need to be made in a factory? Why do you think the people of the Solomon Islands did not use the abundant cowrie shells for money?

3. Develop a currency that you can use in your own house instead of money. Can you perform certain chores for family members for this currency and then trade it for certain things that you want?

Shell Valentine

When whaling was big business in the mid-19th century, sailors often returned home with valentines for their sweethearts or wives. These valentines were not the lacy paper kind but rather hinged, octagonal shadow boxes filled with intricate and beautiful shell designs. Whether made by the sailors themselves or local island women, these valentines became cherished gifts. Here's how to make one that you can hang in your room.

What You Need
- Square greeting card box with clear plastic lid
- Acrylic paints

- Paintbrush
- A variety of shells
- Tacky glue (available at craft supply stores)
- Clear packing tape
- Ribbon

What You Do

1. Remove the lid from your box and set it aside. Paint the sides of the box, inside and outside, with whatever color you wish. Allow the paint to dry.

2. Sailors' valentines often had a heart in the center of the box made out of one or more shells. Pick out a shell or shells that you want to be the focus of your own valentine.

3. Work on the design of your valentine by starting at the center and working your way out. What shells can form the base for your center shell? Lay them out in the center of your box. Don't use any glue yet.

4. Next, pick shells that will form a circle or square around the middle shells. Continue placing shells in your circle or square pattern until you reach the sides of the box. Place a border with another type of shell.

5. After you have laid out all of your shells, it's time to begin gluing them to the box. Begin this time with the border and work your way to the center of your box.

6. Place the clear box lid back on the box after the glue has dried. Tape the sides closed with the clear packing tape.

7. Tape the ribbon to the back of the box to create a loop for hanging your sailor's box. Give your finished valentine to someone special. They'll really love it!

Add ribbon last.

Beautiful Sand

There is nothing like feeling warm, soft sand in between your toes. It is definitely worth taking your shoes off for! Did you ever notice that the sand on different beaches feels different under your feet and might even be different colors? Beach sand is created by the weathering and decomposition of rocks, shells, coral, and other materials. Depending on where the beach is, different matter is worn down by winds and rain. Beaches in parts of Hawaii and Italy have black sand that contains bits of volcanic rock. Other beaches have sand that is a yellow color, which is caused by tiny pieces of quartz. Coral makes pink or white sand on some beaches.

Sand is carried to the ocean from the land by rivers. Sand is brought up to the ocean surface by currents and tides and dropped off on the beach by waves. Sand is also formed by the decomposition of shells and other ocean creatures. Each time you step on a shell at a sand beach, you help to create more sand as you crush tiny shell particles with your feet.

You can start a sand collection from the different beaches you visit. Fill an old film canister (clear ones are best) with beach sand and label it with the beach's name and location. When you get home you can put it in a glass jar. As your collection grows, you'll notice the amazing variety of sand from the beaches you visit.

The Life of a Dune

The beach can be separated into different areas. There is the *subtidal* zone, where the water still covers the sand at low tide, the *intertidal* zone, which is covered by water only during the high tide, the dune area, and the upper beach. The *dune area* is the beach area that is dry all of the time. It begins right after the intertidal area and is a ridge or mound of wind-blown sand. The *upper beach* is dune area and the sandy area beyond, and it is dry all the time.

The dune area is like a desert. In fact, dunes are found in deserts and other areas besides beaches. Beach

dunes, however, form a unique environment. Temperatures in the sand can reach 120 degrees Fahrenheit (49 degrees Celsius) or more. The kinds of plants that can grow on a dune are reduced by the salt in the air and the temperature. The plants that do grow on the dunes adapt to this harsh beach environment. Some adapt with broad leaves that are tough enough to withstand the winds and salt sprays of the ocean. Many of these plants have flexible stems that bend easily in the wind. Some, such as the Indian blanket flower, have hairy

leaves that trap moisture. These plants all have one thing in common—a far-reaching root system that is able to absorb any moisture. These roots also are important because they help to hold the shoreline in place and keep it from eroding.

You will find that many dune areas are protected areas that you will not be allowed to walk on. This protects this fragile area and helps to keep our beaches healthy so that we can all enjoy them.

Stepping off the Beach

Are you ready for a little excitement now? What is the scariest creature found in the ocean? If you said shark, thousands of people would agree with you. Are sharks really that scary? Let's find out.

8

Beware Sharks!

Have you ever heard the music from the movie *Jaws* or visited the movie set? Just hearing the music will send shivers down the spines of many people who saw the movie about the man-eating great white shark. Did the movie give sharks a bad rap? Perhaps. It focused on one very nasty great white shark, but there are actually 350 species of sharks in the ocean that range in size from the pygmy, which is less than 10 inches (25.4 centimeters) long, to the whale shark, which can measure 50 feet (15.24 meters) in length. Sharks are definitely fish to be reckoned with, but no matter how much we might fear them, they do deserve our respect and protection. Protection? Yes, protection! There are many shark populations, such as the great white, that actually need protection from us. These kings of the food chain are slowly disappearing from the ocean waters.

Find out why as you enter into the ocean waters where sharks are king. Don't get worried, though, because here you don't need a shark cage for protection!

More than Teeth!

Teeth are a large part of a shark's character, but let's find out some other things about sharks before looking at their teeth. Remember, a shark is a type of fish, but unlike other fish, sharks have no true bones. Instead, a shark's skeleton is made of cartilage. *Cartilage* is a connective tissue that we also have in our bodies; however, we have a skeleton made of bones. Feel your ear. What you feel in your ear that makes your ear firm is cartilage. That cartilage is the same stuff that forms a shark's body.

Sharks are different from bony fish in other ways as well. Most fish have a gill on each side of their body. Sharks, on the other hand, have between five and seven gills on each side of their body. Bony fish often produce thousands of babies each time they breed, but sharks bear very few young. For example, a blue shark gives birth to about 30 young at a time. That may seem like a lot to us, but not compared to the thousands that a bristle-mouth fish produces. Think about these things as you read on about sharks.

The Monstrous Megalodon

It is because of the shark's cartilage skeleton that there are very few fossils of sharks. The cartilage doesn't last over the years like bone. In spite of this, scientists have found fossilized evidence of sharks that lived 350 million years ago. They have even learned that sharks have not changed all that much in the last 65 million years.

Take a trip to Venice, Florida, and you can get an idea of what one of these early sharks may have looked like. Huge teeth, about four to eight inches (10.16 to 20.32 centimeters) in length, can often be found off the beaches near Venice. These teeth belonged to the predecessor of the great white shark, the Carcharodon megalodon. This big old granddaddy of the great white grew to be between 50 and 100 feet (15.24 and 30.48 meters) in length. Can you imagine a shark that big?

Sandpaper Shark

Sharks have a tough gray skin that is rough and scaly. Their scales are not flat like other fish scales. They are sharp and shaped like teeth. These little scales are called *denticles* and make the skin feel a bit like sandpaper. Here's how you can make your own sandpaper shark.

What You Need
- Gray, fine sandpaper
- Pencil

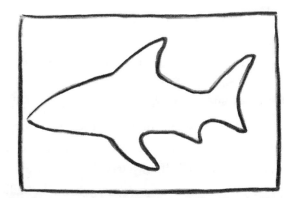

smooth side of sandpaper

- Scissors
- Black marker

What You Do

1. Turn your piece of sandpaper over so that the rough side is facing down.

2. Begin drawing your shark on the smooth side. It will help if you take a look at a picture of a shark while you're drawing.

3. Use the scissors to cut out your shark. When you have finished cutting out your picture, flip it over to see your shark.

4. Add any extra details, such as eyes and teeth, with your black marker.

Smell Experiment

Sharks have a tremendous sense of smell. They can smell very small amounts of substances in the ocean. In fact, sharks can smell one drop of a substance, such as blood, in a million parts of ocean water, and some shark species, such as the great white, can sometimes even detect one part blood per billion parts of ocean water. A shark can be hundreds of meters away from a smell and know exactly where it is coming from. To see how keen a shark's sense of smell is, try this experiment.

What You Need

- Eyedropper
- Oil of peppermint
- 2 8-ounce (237 milliliters) cups
- Liquid measuring cup
- Water
- A friend or grown-up to help

1 drop of oil only

eyedropper

oil of peppermint

What You Do

1. Fill the eyedropper with the oil of peppermint.

2. Squeeze out one drop of the oil into one of the cups. Place your nose in the cup and smell the oil. How does it smell?

3. Measure out 8 ounces (237 milliliters) of water and add it to the cup. Add 8 ounces (237 milliliters) of water to the other cup.

4. Have a friend or grown-up mix up the cups so that you will not know which one has the drop of oil in it.

5. Close your eyes and have the friend or grown-up hold each cup up to your nose. Sniff the water in each cup. Can you tell which cup contains the oil of peppermint?

6. If you'd like, try the experiment again by placing a drop of peppermint oil in a bathtub half filled with water. Can you smell the oil in the water? Are you surprised a shark can?

A Tooth Fairy's Dream

Teeth, teeth, and more teeth! Catch a smiling shark and you will see a mouthful of pearly whites. Sharks are a tooth fairy's dream. Their teeth do not have roots like ours, which means that their teeth are not held into their jaws as tightly as ours are. This means that sharks lose their teeth constantly. Fortunately, sharks have rows of teeth, so that when a tooth falls out while they are eating, another moves up from the next row to fill in the spot.

Not all sharks have the same number of teeth, the same shape of teeth, or the same number of rows of teeth in their mouths. A megamouth shark, for example, has the most rows of teeth. Most sharks have between 5 and 15 rows of teeth. The megamouth can have more than 100 rows of teeth in its upper and lower jaws. It also has the mouth to hold them. The megamouth shark's mouth is about three feet wide and about three feet deep.

The nurse shark has small teeth that are shaped like little cones, which are just right for crushing the shells of clams and crabs. To help the nurse shark find food on the bottom of the ocean are two things that look like fangs on each side of their mouth. Actually, they are sensory structures, called *barbells*, that help this shark detect food, not two more teeth!

The largest shark of all, the whale shark, which grows to about 60 feet (18.29 meters) long and has a mouth that can be 5 feet (1.52 meters) long, actually has little tiny bumps for teeth. Surprising? Not if you knew what this huge shark eats. The whale shark eats krill and other tiny marine organisms that it filters as it swims. So, you can't always judge a book by its cover, can you?

It's Hammer Time

Not all sharks have sleek, torpedo-shaped bodies. Hammerhead sharks are a perfect example. There are nine different species of hammerheads, which have names like bonnethead and winghead. Most make their home in warm temperate waters and tropical coastal areas. They can be as small as 5 feet (1.52 meters) or as large as 19.5 feet (5.94 meters). Hammerhead sharks usually form groups or schools. Some schools can have as many as 100 sharks swimming together. Look at a picture of a hammerhead and you will see that the eyes of the hammerhead are not in the middle of its head but on the

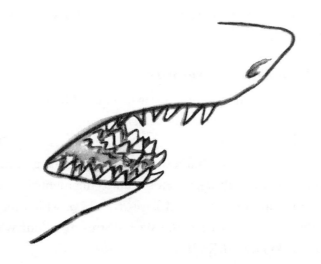

ends of each hammer. Do you think this helps the hammerhead to see around its body? It sure does. To help it even further, the hammerhead swings its head from side to side.

A Whale of a Shark

At a length of at least 40 feet (12.2 meters) long and weighing 13 tons (11.8 metric tons), the whale shark is the largest fish in the world. Like whales, whale sharks feed by filtering plankton from the water. Once in a while, a school of small fish or a stray larger fish is captured by the huge mouth of the whale shark and eaten, but its main food is the plankton.

Dakuwaga, the Fiji Shark God

The people of Fiji tell the story of the fierce god Dakuwaga. In this version, Dakuwaga guarded the reef entrance to the islands. He liked to change himself into the form of a shark and fight all the other reef guards.

After one such day of fighting, Dakuwaga had a great struggle with the guard of the reef at Suva. In this struggle great waves rolled in the mouth of the river and flooded the valleys for many miles. Even so, Dakuwaga was victorious.

Sharing his tales of victory with his old friend, Masilaca, another shark god, he learned that the gods guarding the island of Kadavu had great strength. Wanting the challenge, Dakuwaga quickly left for the island. When he arrived there he found a giant octopus guarding the passage. The arms of the octopus were steadfastly holding onto the coral of the reef. Dakuwaga began to proceed anyway. Soon he found himself in the grip of the octopus, which had wrapped its arms around the shark. Dakuwaga realized that he was in much danger. He began to beg the octopus to release him. He promised the octopus that if he released him that he would never harm any of the Fiji people of Kadavu.

The octopus released Dakuwaga, who kept his promise. Even today the people of Kadavu do not have any fear when they fish at night.

More Shark Legends

Sharks appear in many other legends. The native people of Hawaii tell of the shark god Kamohoalii, who would lead sailors back home when lost at sea. The Maori people say that a shark, caught by the god Maui when he was fishing, was tossed into the night sky. They call the area of the sky *Mango-Roa-I-Ata*, which means "the long shark at dawn." We call this area (our whole night sky) the *Milky Way*.

The Food Chain Game

A necklace is made up of many links, which together create a strong chain. What do you think would happen if one of the links of the chain broke? The ocean is filled with many different food chains. For example, the first link of the chain might be plankton, the second a tiny fish, the third an even bigger fish, and so on until the last link is a huge shark. Let's play the food chain game and see what happens to the different links.

What You Need
* Self-adhesive labels
* Marker
* Spool of twine (several feet in length)
* 5 or 6 players

What You Do

1. Each player gets to play one link of the food chain. On each label write a different link of the food chain. Include plankton, tiny fish, bigger fish, seal, and shark. Also pick a disaster, such as overfishing or illness, for one link.

2. Hand each player a label and have the player stick it on his or her shirt.

3. The players should then line up in order of how they fit into the food chain. Shark should be in the front, followed by seal, bigger fish, tiny fish, and lastly, plankton.

4. The shark player should hold the end of the spool of twine and then pass it to the next person in line, until everyone is holding onto the twine in a row.

5. The player that is playing the disaster then comes and tags one of the players. The tagged player then squats down, still holding the twine, and takes that link out of the chain.

6. Any player that feels the tug of the twine when the player squats down should then also squat. Players who feel that second tug should then squat as well. What happens to the food chain? What do you think happens in the ocean when one of the members of a food chain dies or becomes endangered? Talk it over with the players and try the game again with the disaster player tagging a different link of the food chain.

Sharks Get Souped!

Can you believe that soup may be contributing to the diminished population of sharks? It's true. The demand in Asia for shark fin soup, a delicacy, is causing a lot of controversy among environmentalists who are attempting to rescue shark populations. The soup, made from boiling fins with vinegar, starch, and spices, costs up to $100 a bowl. Restaurants will pay up to $1,066 per pound ($2,350 per kilogram) in Singapore and Hong Kong for shark fins. It is estimated that 100 million sharks, skates, and rays are killed each year, with many of those sharks killed for their fins. This has outraged environmentalists and others who campaign against the soup. Even Hong Kong's popular movie star, Tony Leung, is urging Asians to avoid this delicacy.

Environmentalists are also outraged by how the shark fins are collected. Often, fishermen cut the fins off of a live shark and then throw the shark back into the ocean, where it soon dies. This practice, known as *finning*, is illegal in U.S. waters and is under scrutiny in many other parts of the world.

Jaws *Author Fights to Save Sharks*

Sharks have really had a tough time since *Jaws* was published over 25 years ago. Now the author of *Jaws*, Peter Benchley, is joining the crusade to protect them. Scientists know so much more about sharks now than when Benchley wrote this book. They have learned that many shark attacks occur when the shark mistakes the person for another ocean creature. Find out more about Peter Benchley's shark crusade on-line. You'll find the Web site in the resources section.

Eugenie Clark, Ocean Hero

Dr. Eugenie Clark, otherwise known as the "Shark Lady," is truly an ocean hero. She was honored in 1986 as an ocean hero for the 1984–1985 Year of the Ocean. That in itself would give her the distinction of being an ocean hero, but it is for her countless hours spent with sharks in the effort to study them that she has really distinguished herself.

Dr. Clark is a person who studies fish in the ocean, called an *ichthyologist*. When she is not in the water she teaches in the department of zoology at the University of Maryland. Born in 1922, Dr. Clark was taught to swim at the age of two. At age nine she visited the New York Aquarium. This is where her interest in sharks and the ocean began. Dr. Clark began college at Hunter College in New York when she was only 16 years old.

She later earned her Ph.D. from nearby New York University.

She has conducted 71 dives to study sharks and other sea creatures. On one trip, she discovered a female whale shark caught in Taiwan with 300 shark embryos inside it. Up until that time, it was unknown that any shark species had more than a few babies at one time. Her latest studies have focused on the behavior of deep-sea sharks and tropical sand fishes. She has authored 12 articles about her firsthand research with sharks in *National Geographic* magazine and has truly earned her title of the "Shark Lady."

On to Even Bigger Things

Sharks are not the only large creatures of the sea. There are some even bigger. So, let's go on and have a whale of a time with some more activities.

Have a Whale 9
of a Time

Take a boat ride off the coast of Florida and you might find your boat followed by a group of playful dolphins. Sail in the waters of New England or California and you might spy a spout of water from a whale. Sit on the beach of Baja, California, and you don't even need binoculars to see the pods of whales in the distance. Of all the creatures of the ocean, these are most like us. They are mammals, their communication is highly developed, and they have many of our social traits.

Think about the whales and dolphins you've seen in movies, such as the whale in *Free Willy* or the dolphin, Flipper. There are so many stories of whales and dolphins and we're still learning about these fascinating creatures.

A Whale by Any Other Name

Whales, along with dolphins and porpoises, are mammals called *cetacea*. There are three groups of cetaceans: [1] *archaeoceti*, which are extinct, [2] *odontoceti*, which are toothed whales and include dolphins, porpoises, beluga whales, and the pilot whale, and [3] *mysticeti*, which are the baleen whales and include the humpback whale, gray whale, and right whale.

Just like us, whales need air to breathe. They must rise to the surface of the water to breathe through their blowholes, which are found on the tops of their heads. Like all other mammals, whales are warm-blooded and have live babies. What else do you think we have in common with them?

The Blowhole

When a whale is underwater, its blowhole is shut. When the whale comes to the surface of the water to breathe,

it first breathes out, or exhales, through the blowhole. That "blow" is the mist of spray that you can sometimes see from a beach or on a whale-watching cruise. It can be seen miles away from the whale. The whale then breathes in through the blowhole and goes back under the water. Toothed whales have one blowhole, while baleen whales have two, just as we have two nostrils.

Baleen or Toothed?

Whales eat a variety of foods. Some whales feed on fish, while others feed on plankton. Which ones do you think feed on fish? Which ones on plankton? If you guessed that toothed whales feed on fish and baleen whales feed on plankton, you are right!

Baleen acts like a big, fringed brush that hangs in the whale's mouth. Whales that have baleen open their mouths as they swim, allowing seawater to flow inside their mouths. The baleen traps the plankton and other tiny tasty creatures inside the mouths of the whales. They then spit out the water after it has passed through the baleen. Baleen whales include the gray, right, and humpback whales.

Other whales have teeth. Killer whales, dolphins, belugas, and other toothed whales feed on fish in the ocean. Dolphins catch their slippery prey with their teeth and often swallow them whole. Other whales chew up their fish, squid, or cuttlefish with their teeth.

Ocean Notion
Why do you suppose whales have blowholes on the tops of their heads? Think about how you must come up for air when you are swimming underwater. How much of your head must come out of the water for you to take a breath? How much of the whale's head must come out of the water for it to breathe?

A Whale's Fingerprint

Take a look at your finger. Your finger has a distinct pattern, called a *fingerprint*. A fingerprint can be used to identify a person because each fingerprint is unique. Humpback whales and gray whales don't have fingers or fingerprints but can often be identified by looking at their tails. The patterns of white color, scars, and scratches are different for each tail and provide researchers with a way to identify each whale. This enables the researchers to keep records on each whale they're observing.

The White One

Did you grow up listening to Raffi sing the song "Baby Beluga"? Well, it's time to pull out the record again and sing along. The beluga whale, whose name is derived from the Russian word *belukha*, meaning "white," lives among the ice in the Arctic Ocean and the seas adjoining it. Do you think it helps the whale to be white? Beluga whales are not born white, however. Baby belugas are gray. They turn white as adults. What do you think might eat beluga whales? Beluga whales fall prey to killer whales and polar bears in the Arctic. Belugas don't swim very fast, only two to five miles (3.22 to 8.05 kilometers) per hour.

The beluga is known as the "sea canary" because it is so vocal. Belugas make at least 11 different vocal sounds, including trills, chirps, mews, clucks, whistles, and squeals. See if you can make 11 different sounds.

Moby Click

Like other toothed whales, the beluga whale uses sound to locate food. The whale sends out a clicking sound that moves through the water until it bounces off something. The sound then travels back to the whale and the whale is able to tell how far away the something is. Not only is this important for locating food, but the echoes also help beluga whales to find breathing holes in the Arctic ice.

This process of sending out sound and listening for echoes is called *echolocation*. Can you think of another animal that uses echolocation to find food? Here are a few hints:

1. It flies through the air at night.
2. It feeds on insects.
3. It likes to hang upside down.

Do you know what kind of animal I am?

~~~~~~~~~~~~~~~~~~~~~~~~

Ocean Notion
What do you call a group of whales? Not a herd, a smack, or a gaggle, but a *pod*.

~~~~~~~~~~~~~~~~~~~~~~~~

Echolocation Game

Test out echolocation with your friends and this new game.

What You Need
➤ Open area to play
➤ Blindfold
➤ Chairs for each player
➤ 4 or more players

What You Do
1. Blindfold the first player. Position the chairs in a random pattern around the room.
2. Each of the remaining players sits in a chair.
3. The object of the game is for the blindfolded "whale" to reach the other side of the room, while avoiding walking into any of the chairs.
4. The whale starts out on one side of the room and begins to walk across the room making a clicking noise.
5. When the whale starts to walk toward a chair, the player in that chair begins repeating the clicking noise back to the blindfolded player, just as if it is returning the echo from the whale. Can the whale make it to the other side of the room without bumping into any of the chairs?
6. Blindfold another player then change the chairs around. See if the new whale can get to the other side of the room without bumping into any of the chairs.

whistles, clicks, and cries. Test out your own hearing skills with this activity.

What You Need
- Blindfold
- Whistle and other assorted noisemakers
- 2 or more players

What You Do

1. Find a quiet room where you can play this game. Blindfold the first player.

2. The others should each go to a different spot in the room and one by one make a sound with the whistle or something else, such as tapping a pencil on a table.

3. After each sound, the blindfolded player should try to identify the sound and where it came from in the room. Take turns being the blindfolded player. Who can identify the most sounds? Can you tell where each of the sounds came from?

Whale Talk

The squeaks and clicks that whales produce not only help them find food but also help them communicate with each other. Some of these sounds can travel for hundreds of miles in the ocean water! The songs and sounds of the whales have become the inspiration for movies, such as *Star Trek IV*, stories, and above all, music. Some groups, such as the Paul Winter Consort, blend the sounds of whales into their music.

Can you tell the difference among many different sounds as whales can? They can discriminate among

Origami Whale

There have been songs, paintings, sculptures, and stories inspired by whales. Try your hand at creating a whale using the ancient Japanese art of origami.

What You Need

→ Square sheet of thin paper

→ Flat working area

→ Scissors

→ Marker

What You Do

1. Fold the square in half diagonally so that you have a triangle. Unfold the paper on a flat surface so that the fold is horizontal to you.

2. Fold the bottom right-hand side up to meet the fold and the top right-hand side down to meet the fold. Keep the paper in the same position.

3. Fold the point on the left side over to meet the two other folds. The new fold should look like a small triangle.

4. Fold the paper along the first fold mark you made.

5. You should now begin to see the form of your whale. Fold the pointed tail up.

6. Using the scissors, make a small cut in the fold of the tail and turn down the edges.

7. Complete your whale by drawing eyes and fins with the marker.

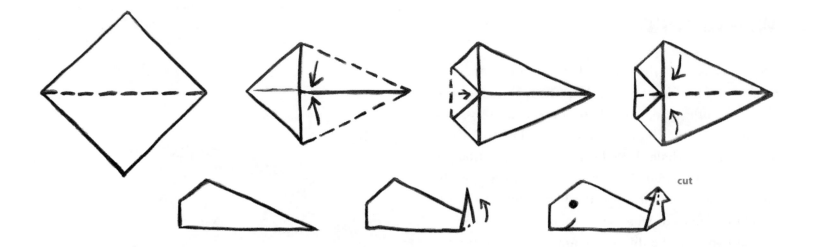

cut

Narwhal, the Unicorn Myth

Have you ever seen a picture of a unicorn? The most obvious difference between a unicorn and an ordinary horse is its large horn growing out of its forehead. Do you think unicorns are real? During the Middle Ages, people would see such horns being sold at fairs. These horns were believed to hold magical properties, and many people imagined the animal that they came from as the unicorn that you have probably seen in pictures. The animal that the horns actually came from was the narwhal. Most people had never heard of this whale during that time.

The narwhal is a whale that has a huge tusk growing out of its forehead, just like the imagined unicorn. It lives in the cold seas way up north in the Arctic waters. Narwhals have been hunted by Inuit hunters for their skin, meat, and tusks.

Scientists are still not quite sure why these whales have the tusks. They had thought that maybe they used them to spear fish or break holes in ice, but those ideas proved to be wrong. What do you think?

Killer Whales

Sea World gave us a new look at the orca whale with the star of their whale show, Shamu. The black-and-white coloration pattern of the orca makes it easy to identify. The orca, also known as the killer whale, eats everything from small fish to whales that dwarf their size. They have no natural predators. But don't worry, you have nothing to fear from these killer whales because they don't eat people!

The Gift of the Whale, an Inuit Tale

This version of this Inuit tale sets out to explain the relationship between the Inuit hunters and the whales they depended on for food.

The Great Spirit created the land with many good things. He created the sun, moon, and stars. He created the mountains and the ocean, the fish and the birds, the seals and the great bears. After creating it all he decided to make one more thing. He then created the Bowhead Whale. It was very fine. The Bowhead sang as it swam through the ocean. It was in perfect balance with all around it.

The Great Spirit saw all of this. He also saw that the Inuit people needed the whale to survive. They needed the flesh of the whale to eat and keep them warm. And so the Great Spirit gave the Bowhead to the Inuit. Each spring the whales would come to the surface to be hunted by the Inuit. They would come as long as the Inuit took only what they needed to survive. Even so, the Great Spirit made a thick cloud to hang above the ice at this time so that he would not have to watch the hunt of his great Bowhead.

Then and Now: "Thar She Blows"

Whales have been hunted for more than one thousand years, but whaling really became a major industry in the 19th century. By 1846 there were more than 700 American whaling ships on the high seas. Both men and boys left their homes for life on the sea. They put up with maggot-infested food and other terrible conditions for sometimes months at a time. As soon as a whale spout was spotted, the cry "Thar she blows!" would be heard on deck. The skipper would yell back, "Where away?" and "What d'ye call her?" The whale and its location would then be identified and the chase would commence.

In those days, whales were harpooned. Sometimes boats would be smashed by the weight of the fighting whale and often men drowned. In the end, the baleen was used for corsets (girdles for women) and brushes, the blubber for meat, the oil for candles, and the bone and teeth for decoration.

The 20th century finally brought a decrease in commercial whaling but not before thousands of whales were killed with high-powered harpoons from steam-powered boats. In 1988 a worldwide ban on killing whales went into effect and may have saved some species from becoming extinct. Even so, the crusade to save the whales is not over.

Ocean Notion

Elian Gonzales arrived in the United States on Thanksgiving Day. He spent roughly 50 hours lashed to an inner tube in shark-infested waters off the coast of Florida after his boat sank. In a later interview with Diane Sawyer, young Elian drew a picture of himself in the inner tube, the boat, and a dolphin. When asked if he saw any sharks, he said, "There were only dolphins around me." He claimed that every time he began to slip beneath the waves because he couldn't hold on any longer, the dolphins would push him back up.

There have been many reports of dolphin rescues over the years. In fact, the Annam people of Indonesia call the dolphin *Ba Ngu*, the goddess who rescues sailors.

Dolphins Help During War

Perhaps the most unlikely soldiers of war, dolphins, known for their intelligence and friendliness, have played a part in the Vietnam War and Persian Gulf War under the auspices of the U.S. Navy. In 1960 the navy began a program called the Marine Mammal Program. The navy had two goals for the program. The first was to study the echolocation and speed of dolphins and beluga whales in order to design better ways of locating objects under the water by using sonar and to help increase the speed of its boats. The second goal was to train dolphins, beluga whales, and other marine mammals to carry out underwater jobs for the navy.

Marine mammals proved to be very helpful to the navy. Bottlenose dolphins were used to locate underwater enemy mines and mark them so that the navy could avoid or remove them. They were also used to protect navy boats that were anchored in the ocean during the Vietnam War and the Persian Gulf War. The dolphins were trained to patrol the areas around the boats.

Navy dolphins have not stopped their military service. Even in times of peace, these dolphins have been employed to help clean the ocean of old mines and other munitions. Just recently, U.S. Navy dolphins took part in a NATO exercise called "Blue Game," the purpose of which was to locate and clear some of the 80,000 mines deployed off the Norwegian coast by the Nazis during World War II. These mines and other wartime debris pose a threat to fishermen and divers in the area.

Pink Dolphins

Can you imagine a place where there would be pink dolphins? Pink dolphins sound like something right out of the pages of a fairy tale, don't they? Well, they're not. They're right here on Earth! Specifically, in the Amazon River. Capillaries close to the surface of the dolphin's skin account for the pinkish tinge in the color of the dolphin.

The pink river dolphins live in murky water and therefore do not use their sight as much as echolocation to locate food. They are found to have much smaller eyes than other dolphins. Aside from their pink color, they also have other characteristics that make them look different than most dolphins. They have a hump instead of a dorsal fin on their back and a long beak.

Ocean Notion

Which ocean mammal do you think is the fastest swimmer? The dolphin is the fastest marine mammal. It can travel up to 22 miles (35.4 kilometers) per hour and even faster when being pushed along while swimming at the bow of a boat.

Different Places

Whales and dolphins inhabit everything from icy seas to warm rainforest rivers. Many of the creatures we have covered so far have lived in the warmer parts of the ocean. It's time to travel on to those icy seas where the beluga lives to find out what other creatures brave the cold waters of the polar oceans.

Travel Icy Seas and Glaciers

10

Imagine a world filled with white snow and cold, icy water. It is a world where there is ice that never melts. The animals have thick coats and warm blubber to keep warm, big eyes and sharp hearing for dark water, and flippers and streamlined bodies for efficient swimming. You might think that there can't be much life in these icy seas, but you'd be wrong. Penguins, polar bears, and puffins are just some of the critters that make their homes in the icy polar seas.

The Inuit Tale of Sedna, Goddess of the Sea

The sea is extremely important to the people of the Arctic. Just like the people that live on islands in warmer climates, the people in the Arctic rely on the sea for food and transportation. Wherever the sea holds that much importance in a culture, stories and mythology evolve. This is a version of an Inuit tale told by people who live in the Arctic region of Canada and Alaska.

Sedna was a beautiful Inuit girl. She was so beautiful that she thought she was too beautiful to marry just anyone, so she continued to turn down any hunters that came wanting to marry her. After a long time of this, her father said to her, "Sedna, you must marry soon. We are in need of food, and you must have a husband now to take care of you. You must marry the next hunter who comes to ask for your hand in marriage."

Sedna refused to listen to her father and continued to gaze at herself in the sea. Soon a hunter arrived at their camp. He was dressed in wonderful furs and appeared to have done very well for himself. Sedna's father told the hunter that his wonderful daughter would make a good wife for him. The hunter saw Sedna and agreed to marry her. She traveled with the hunter to his camp but was not happy.

After many days with the hunter, Sedna's father felt very sad. He believed that he could hear Sedna's cries in the harsh Arctic winds and decided to rescue her. When he reached the camp he found Sedna standing on the shore watching for him. She quickly jumped in the kayak with her father and the two paddled away from the hunter.

They traveled for many hours and were getting very tired. It was then that Sedna looked up into the sky and saw a black spot overhead. She knew it must be her angry husband searching for her. Her husband had turned himself into a black raven. He flew at the kayak and tormented the two in the boat. Her father swung his paddle at the raven, but the bird kept swooping down upon them. In the next moment the raven dove down near the water so that its wing touched the wave before it flew up again toward the sky. Just as its wing touched the wave a terrible storm began to blow.

The storm tossed the kayak back and forth until Sedna found herself in the water. The icy water began to freeze her, and her fingers soon broke off. They floated down into the water and became whales, seals, and other sea animals. The cold finally took over Sedna and she began to sink into the sea, but she did not die. Sedna became the goddess of the sea. Her friends are the seals and the whales. Sometimes, when she feels very angry, the sea becomes violent and stormy. Hunters know they must treat her well, which is why hunters drop water into the mouths of the seals they catch—to thank Sedna for helping them feed their families.

The Inuit people tell the story of Sedna, goddess of the sea, in their mythology, but other cultures have different stories. In Roman mythology, Neptune is known as the god of the sea. Ancient Greeks told tales of Poseidon, the god of the sea. Take a look at some of these other myths. Are there any similarities? Differences?

What Is a Glacier?

Glaciers are moving masses of ice that don't melt from year to year. The movement of glaciers has a great effect on the land around and underneath them. In fact, the spectacular fjords in Norway were created by the movement of glaciers. There are glaciers in Norway that continue to grow. The Folgefonn glacier in northern Norway grows at a rate of about 6 feet (1.8 meters) per day. The Jostedalsbreen glacier can grow up to 100 meters every year. They also move, like all glaciers.

Norway is not the only place to find glaciers. There are between 70,000 and 200,000 glaciers in the world. They begin in snowfields, and many extend into the sea. Glaciers store about three-fourths of the earth's freshwater. The largest glacier is larger than the whole country of Belgium. The Jostedal glacier in Norway is the largest glacier in Europe and can be up to 500 feet (152.4 meters) thick in some parts.

Icebergs

An iceberg is formed when a part of the edge of a glacier or ice sheet breaks off into the water. Only about 10 percent of the iceberg is visible above the water. The rest is below. Icebergs look like ice mountains. Have you heard of the oceanliner named the *Titanic*? The *Titanic* sank because it hit an iceberg. The Southern Ocean around Antarctica is filled with floating icebergs that have broken off from ice sheets.

Life on the Ice

Penguins make their homes among the ice and cold of the Antarctic. These birds are only found south of the equator. There are 17 species of penguins in the Southern Hemisphere. Penguins can't fly like most birds. Instead, they fly through the water at speeds up to seven miles (11.27 kilometers) per hour. Their bodies are shaped like torpedoes, which helps them move efficiently through the water. Penguins are also able to leap right out of the water onto the ice. They are a bit awkward out of the water as they waddle along on the ice but can instantly transform themselves into toboggans and swoosh over the snow on their bellies. Have you ever watched playful penguins at an aquarium? They are a lot of fun to watch!

Father's Day Is Every Day

Emperor penguin males take on an important role in the lives of their chicks. After the female lays her egg, she passes it to the male. The male then takes over the egg's incubation by balancing the egg on his feet. The egg stays nice and warm nestled in the male's thick skin and feathers. Where is the female during all of this? All the females go off to feed after they lay their eggs. The males all huddle together to keep warm and to protect their eggs during their incubation period. It takes nine weeks for the eggs to hatch. The males don't eat until their eggs hatch. As you can probably guess, they will have lost a bit of weight by the time the females return to take over. While the female begins her care of her new chick, the male heads out to find his own food. Now that's shared parenting!

Emperor penguins and chick

The Great White Bear

It may not have influenced the name of the Arctic, but this bear definitely rules the Arctic. Up north, far away from the land of the penguins, the polar bear makes its home amid the ice and snow. It feeds on small beluga whales, seals, and anything else it can get its paws on. This bear has no boundaries. In fact, it can even swim long distances, which is why the Latin name for this bear is *ursus maritimus*, or "sea bear." It moves across the ice and water from Alaska all the way to Russia by way of Canada, Greenland, and northern Norway. The International Agreement for the Conservation of Polar Bears, created in 1973, set out to protect the polar bear populations in these countries. Since then, the Norwegian population of polar bears has nearly doubled in size. Even with this agreement, native people in

Ocean Notion

The Arctic gets its name from the Greek word *arktos*. Can you guess what this word might mean? Here's a hint: What do Winnie-the-Pooh, Paddington, and teddy have in common? There are all bears! *Arktos* is the Greek word for bear. You'd think it was named for the king of the ice, the polar bear, but actually it's named for the northern constellation of the bear.

Canada, Alaska, Russia, and Greenland are given the right to continue their tradition of hunting polar bears. They kill over 700 bears each year.

Carve a Soapstone Polar Bear

Soapstone is an easy-to-carve stone that is used for sculptures all over the world. Native people in the Arctic use soapstone to carve the animals that they see in their lives. They carve whales, seals, walruses, and polar bears. Practice your own carving skills using a bar of soap instead of soapstone to make your very own polar bear sculpture.

What You Need

- Bar of rectangular white soap (Ivory brand works well)
- Pencil
- Plastic knife or clay tools
- Black marker
- A grown-up to assist

cut away

What You Do

1. Begin your sculpture by drawing your polar bear on the bar of soap. Use the entire surface for your drawing. This will make it easier for you to carve.

2. Use the knife or clay tools to cut away the areas around your polar bear.

3. Create the details of your sculpture. The serrated edge of the plastic knife can be used to lightly scrape the soap bar to carve hair on your bear. The marker can be used to draw the eyes and nose on your bear.

There's Nothing Like a Mother Bear

Have you ever heard your mom referred to as a mother bear? If you have, that is because mother bears are very protective of their young cubs. Polar bear moms actually fight off larger adult bears if they feel their cubs are in danger. They have also been known to jump at helicopters carrying research scientists when the helicopters were perceived as threats to their young.

Young cubs stay with their moms for about two to three years, depending on how extreme the climate may be. If the cubs survive to adulthood, they have a good chance of living 15 to 18 years, and some have been found in their 30s.

Total Insulation

Polar bears are so well insulated by a thick layer of blubber that they give off no heat. That means that you cannot photograph a polar bear with infrared photography, which records the heat of a subject on film. It also means that it is easy for a polar bear to overheat when it is running and expending a lot of energy.

The heavy white fur that covers and helps insulate the polar bear is not actually white, but transparent. It resembles hollow fishing line. Our eyes see the fur as white, just as we see ice and snow as white.

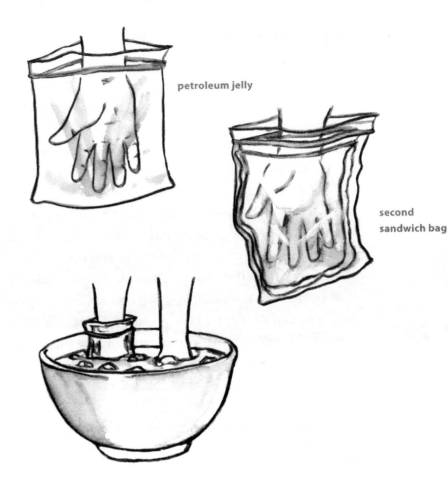

petroleum jelly

second sandwich bag

Blubber Experiment

Do you want to know what it feels like to have a layer of blubber to keep you warm? Check out this simple experiment to find out.

What You Need
➡ 2 plastic sandwich bags
➡ Petroleum jelly or shortening
➡ Spatula
➡ Bowl of ice water

What You Do
1. Place your hand in one of the sandwich bags. Use the spatula to spread the petroleum jelly or shortening all over the outside of the bag. This layer is your blubber. Make sure that you spread a thick layer to form your blubber.

2. Slip the other sandwich bag over the first bag on your hand to make a sleeve for your hand.

3. Place your bare hand and the covered hand in the bowl of ice water. Which one feels colder?

Pinnipeds

The polar bears don't roam on the Arctic ice by themselves. Seals, walruses, and musk oxen also make their homes amid the northern ice and snow. The penguins in the Southern Ocean also share the ice with a few species of seals. Seals and walruses are called *pinnipeds*, meaning that they have flippers instead of limbs. Have you ever seen a seal at a zoo or aquarium? Seals are natural clowns and often star in aquarium shows. But you can bet that you won't find any seals in their natural habitat twirling balls on their noses. The seals that live amid the ice spend their days fishing, lying around, and keeping away from polar bears. They are great divers. The Weddell seal would win the seal Olympics in the diving category hands down. It can dive down about 1,970 feet (600 meters). Consider this: the height of the Empire State Building is 1,454 feet (443.2 meters). Better yet, a seal can stay under the water for over an hour.

Clamdigger

Walruses need a lot of food each day to keep all that weight on. In *Through the Looking Glass* by Lewis Carroll, the Walrus and the Carpenter take a walk with some oysters and then eat them. Actually, walruses prefer clams, and they can be quite inventive in their hunt for them. They use their tusks to anchor themselves to the ground while they're hunting for their meal. They also squirt large, powerful streams of water out of their mouths, which act like drills to get to the clams. With this method, they can eat as many as 3,000 to 6,000 clams in one feeding session!

Here's a fun activity to try that will show you just how much food they eat.

What You Need
- Clam
- Knife (for a grown-up to use to open the clam)
- Kitchen scale
- Calculator
- A grown-up to assist

What You Do

1. A Pacific walrus weighs about 2,000 pounds (907 kilograms) and eats about 60 pounds (27 kilograms) of clams each day. It sucks the clams out of their shells, so you need to find out how much a clam without its shell weighs. Have a grown-up open the clam using the knife. Scoop it out onto the scale. Find out how many clams would make up 1

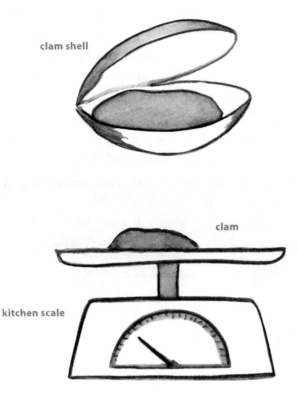

clam shell

clam

kitchen scale

Krill, a Most Important Creature

Perhaps the most important creature in the northern and southern oceans is not the whale or the polar bear or the penguin, but the krill. Krill are tiny shrimplike zooplankton, no bigger than half your finger, but they pack a lot of nutrition for many ocean creatures. Whales, penguins, fish, and seals all feed on krill. People in Norway and Japan also eat krill. The krill stay deep in the dark ocean waters during the day and rise up to the surface to feed on the phytoplankton at night. They travel in large swarms. It is important for krill populations to have clean water with a good balance of phytoplankton in order to survive. They are the important second link in many ocean food chains.

pound by dividing 16 ounces (1 pound) by the weight of the clam.

2. Use your calculator to find out how many clams you would need to place on the scale for it to read 60 pounds. (Sixty pounds is equal to 960 ounces. Divide 960 ounces by the weight of the clam you weighed. This answer equals the total number of clams you would need.)

3. How much do you weigh? How many clams would it take to make up your weight? That's a lot of clams, isn't it?

Spill Solution

Oil spills are a major problem for marine life wherever they happen. In 1989 the Exxon Valdez ran aground in the Prince William Sound of Alaska. It spilled 232,000 barrels of oil into the sound, creating a major ocean disaster. Many otters and birds died as a result. When a bird's feathers become coated in oil, it loses its ability to remain waterproof. The ocean water soaks into the bird and the bird drowns or freezes as a result. Many of the wildlife die from swallowing the poisonous oil. It is estimated that only 8 percent of the oil spilled in that disaster was actually recovered; the rest was dispersed into the environment by the storms of the Arctic.

There are a few ways to clean up oil from the ocean, but none of them are perfect. First the spill is contained by putting up barriers in the water so that it does not spread into other areas. The oil floats on top of the water, creating a layer above the seawater. One way to clean up the oil is to skim it off the surface, another is to soak it up, and another is to try to sink it to the bottom of the ocean.

Investigate the different ways that oil can be cleaned up from the ocean with this activity.

What You Need
- Large dishpan
- Water
- Cooking oil
- Drinking straw
- Sand
- Cotton balls
- Paper towels

What To Do
1. Pour water into the dishpan until it is filled halfway. Pour enough oil to create a layer on top of the water. That's your oil spill.
2. Imagine you are on the task force to clean up this spill. What will you try first?
3. Experiment with the straw, sand, cotton balls, paper towels, and anything else you can think of to remove the oil. What works best? Can you imagine a spill that consists of over 100,000 barrels of oil?

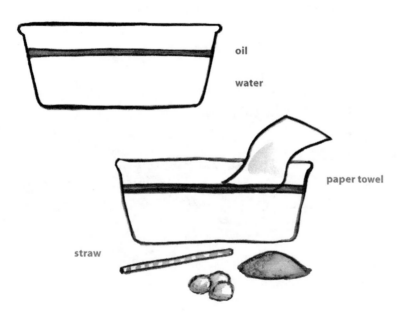

oil

water

paper towel

straw

Sweaters for Penguins

The people of Australia have set out to protect their population of fairy penguins on the island of Tasmania from the effects of an oil spill. The Tasmanian Conservation Trust has gathered 1,000 tiny woolen sweaters for the fairy penguins to wear in case of an oil spill. The sweaters were knit by people as far away as Japan and will prevent the penguins from preening themselves and ingesting the oil. The pattern for the sweaters was based on a pattern previously used for northern seabirds.

Make a Difference

We live at an interesting time. It is a time when technology is available to take us into the far depths of the ocean and yet there is still so much that has yet to be explored and mapped. We have mapped out the moon but have not finished mapping out the ocean floor. It is also a time when more and more people visit or want to live on the shores of the ocean. Each year 35 million people now visit the New Jersey shore. More people enjoy scuba diving, sea kayaking, and bodyboarding than ever. Seafood is a nutritionally important food and has increased in popularity. All of these things affect the balance of our ocean.

It is also a time when people all across the world have increased their concern and activism to protect our living ocean. Its health is up to all of us. There are a number of active organizations that you can join to help protect this important part of our planet. These organizations include the Center for Marine Conservation, the Cousteau Society, and the Waterkeepers, as well as the National Audubon Society, Wildlife Conservation Society, and Greenpeace. Look in the resources section for how to contact them.

Here are some things you can do to help preserve the health of our living ocean.

1. Conserve water. Take shorter showers and baths and don't let the water run while you brush your teeth.

2. Join a local citizens' environmental program.

3. Adopt and clean up a nearby beach or stream.

4. Recycle your paper, bottles, batteries, glass, aluminum, used motor oil, and plastic.

5. Spread the word. Tell your friends about things they can do to help and share the things you've learned in this book with them.

6. Review the other lists in this book for things you can do specifically to help fish, turtles, and coral reefs.

7. Enjoy the beauty of the ocean. Visit it and experience how special it is. Share your love for it with others. Remember, you can make a difference.

Resources

Aquariums Around the United States

California

La Jolla
Birch Aquarium at Scripps
(858) 534-FISH, www.aquarium.ucsd.edu

Long Beach
Aquarium of the Pacific
100 Aquarium Way, Long Beach, CA 90802
(562) 590-3100, www.aquariumofpacific.org

Monterey

Monterey Aquarium

886 Cannery Row, Monterey, CA 93940

(831) 648-4800, www.mbayaq.org

San Francisco

Steinhart Aquarium

(415) 750-7145, www.calacademy.org/aquarium

Connecticut

Mystic

Mystic Aquarium

55 Coogan Boulevard, Mystic, CT

(860) 572-5955, www.mysticaquarium.org

Norwalk

Maritime Aquarium at Norwalk

Water Street, Norwalk, CT

(203) 852-0700, www.maritimeaquarium.org

Florida

Tampa

Florida Aquarium

701 Channelside Drive, Tampa, FL

(813) 273-4000, www.flaquarium.net

Hawaii

Honolulu

Waikiki Aquarium

(808) 923-9741, www.mic.hawaii.edu/aquarium

Waimanalo

Sea Life Park Hawaii

(808) 259-7933,

www.hawaiiweb.com/html/sea_life_park.html

Illinois

Chicago

John G. Shedd Aquarium

Solidarity Drive, Chicago, IL

(312) 939-2435, www.sheddnet.org

Iowa

Des Moines

Aquarium Center

501 E. 30th, Des Moines, IA

(515) 263-0612

Louisiana

New Orleans

Aquarium of the Americas

1 Canal Street, New Orleans, LA 70130

(504) 861-2537, www.auduboninstitute.org

Maine

Portland
Gulf of Maine Aquarium
(207) 772-2321, http://octopus.gma.org

Maryland

Baltimore
National Aquarium in Baltimore
Pier 3, 501 East Pratt Street, Baltimore, MD 21202
(410) 576-3800, www.aqua.org

Massachusetts

Boston
New England Aquarium
Central Warf, Boston, MA
(617) 973-5200, www.neaq.org

Michigan

Detroit
Belle Isle Aquarium
(248) 398-0900, http://detroitzoo.org

New Jersey

Camden
New Jersey State Aquarium
(856) 365-3300, www.njaquarium.org

New Mexico

Albuquerque
Albuquerque Biological Park (including the aquarium)
(505) 764-6200, www.cabq.gov/biopark

New York

Brooklyn, Coney Island
New York Aquarium (Brooklyn)
(718) 265-FISH

Long Island
Atlantis Marine World Aquarium
(631) 208-9200, www.atlantismarineworld.com

North Carolina

North Carolina Aquariums, www.ncaquariums.com
- at **Fort Fisher**, (910) 458-8257
- at **Pine Knoll Shores**, (252) 247-4004
- at **Roanoke Island**, (252) 473-3494

Ohio

Columbus
Columbus Zoo and Aquarium
9990 Riverside Drive, Powell, OH, 43065
(614) 645-3400, www.colszoo.org

Oregon

Newport

Oregon Coast Aquarium

2820 S.E. Ferry Slip Road, Newport, OR 97365

(541) 867-3474, www.aquarium.org

Pennsylvania

Pittsburgh

Pittsburgh Zoo and Aquarium

(412) 665-3640, http://zoo.pgh.pa.us

Tennessee

Chattanooga

Tennessee Aquarium

1 Broad Street, Chattanooga, TN 37401

(800) 262-0695, www.tennis.org

Texas

Dallas

Dallas World Aquarium

1801 N. Griffin Street, Dallas, TX 75202

(214) 720-2224, http://dwazoo.com

Washington

Seattle

Seattle Aquarium

Pier 59, 1483 Alaskan Way, Seattle, WA

(206) 386-4300, www.seattleaquarium.org

More Marine Places to Visit

Here are some other places to visit that are a bit different from aquariums. At these sites you might find a dolphin show or a cove where you can swim with dolphins. At the Bailey-Matthews Shell Museum you will be able to see shells from all over the world. Check these places out and discover some very unique experiences.

UNITED STATES

California

San Diego

Sea World

500 Sea World Drive, San Diego, CA

(619) 226-3901

Florida

Orlando
Discovery Cove
(877) 4-DISCOVERY, www.discoverycove.com

Swim with dolphins and manta rays. Snorkel in a coral reef.

Sea World
7007 Sea World Drive, Orlando, FL
(800) 327-2424

Marineland
Marineland
9600 Ocean Shore Boulevard, Marineland, FL
(888) 279-9194, www.marineland.net

Sanibel Island
Bailey-Matthews Shell Museum
3075 Sanibel-Captiva Drive, Sanibel Island, FL
(888) 679-6450, www.shellmuseum.org

Oregon

Florence
Sea Lion Caves
Coast Highway 101, Florence, OR
(541) 547-3111, www.sealioncaves.com

Visit the world's largest sea cave.

Texas

San Antonio
Sea World
10500 Sea World Drive, San Antonio, TX
(210) 523-3900

INTERNATIONAL

Australia

Tasmania
Seahorse World
Inspection Head Wharf, Beauty Point TAS 7270
P.O. Box 53, Beaconsfield, 7270
wwwseahorseworld.com.au

Canada

Vancouver
Vancouver Aquarium Marine Science Centre
www.vancouver-aquarium.org

England

Dorset
Weymouth Sealife Park
Lodmoor Country Park, Weymouth, Dorset, DT4 7SX
www.weymouth.gov.uk/sealife.htm

Italy

Genoa

Genoa Aquarium

www.acquario.ge.it/Inglese/HOME_E.HTM

The largest aquarium in Europe.

Japan

Osaka

Port of Nagoya Public Aquarium

www.u-net.city.nagoya.jp/ncvb/minatoe.htm#suizoku

Visitors discover the Japan Sea and Pacific and Antarctic oceans.

Norway

Bergen

Bergen Akvariet

(+47) 55 55 71 71, www.akvariet.com

The largest aquarium in Norway. Visitors can see the creatures and plants that live in the Norwegian Sea.

Places to Visit on the Web

Jeff's Nudibranch and Coral Reef Gallery

www.divegallery.com

Amazing reef photographs taken in the Philippine Islands.

Ocean Images Underwater Photography

www.oceanimages.com

Sea and Sky Web

www.seasky.org/mainmenu.html

Check out the Ocean Realm area of this site for some wonderful photographs of ocean life.

Calendar of Ocean Events

January 1 to March 31

Whale Watching in Los Angeles, CA

Take a tour boat out to see visiting gray whales.

January 19

Anniversary of the Arrival of Sea Lions, San Francisco, CA

February

Festival of Whales, Dana Point, CA
Annual monthlong celebration.
Information: www.dpfestivalofwhales.com

February 17

Pacific Whale Foundation's Whale Day Celebration,
Maui, HI
Food, music, crafts, and Parade of Whales.
Information: (800) WHALE-1-1 or
www.pacificwhale.org/news/calendar.html

Late February

Great Whale Count in Maui, HI, sponsored by Pacific Whale
Foundation
Join others in recording sightings of humpback whales. The
2001 count recorded over 952 sightings of humpbacks in a
three-hour period. Information: (800) WHALE-1-1 or
www.pacificwhale.org/news/calendar.html

April 25

Penguin Day
This holiday started years ago to celebrate the penguins'
short migration to feed on krill (tiny shrimplike crustaceans)
100 miles north of their home in the Antarctic.

July

San Clemente Ocean Festival, San Clemente, CA
Annual festival with proceeds donated to ocean
organizations. Information: (949) 440-6141 or
www.oceanfestival.org

July 4

**Turtle Independence Day, Mauna Lani Bay Hotel
Kohala Coast, Big Island, Hawaii**
Three- and four-year-old sea turtles released.
Information: (808) 885-6622

Third Saturday in September

Annual International Coastal Cleanup
Join volunteers for three hours in the largest marine
pollution cleanup effort. The event is sponsored by the
Center for Marine Conservation. Information and regional
coordinators: www.cmc-oceans.org

November 1 to February 28

See manatees in the warm Florida waters.

Favorite Ocean Books, Videos, and Web Sites

Chapter 1: Catch a Wave

Books

Heiligman, Deborah. *The Mysterious Ocean Highway: Benjamin and the Gulf Stream*. Austin, TX: Raintree/Steck Vaughn, 1999.

Kraske, Robert. *The Voyager's Stone: The Adventures of a Message-Carrying Bottle Adrift on the Ocean Sea*. New York: Orchard Books, 1995.

Chapter 2: Enter the Sunlit Zone

Books

Weeks, Sarah. *Follow the Moon*. New York: Harpercollins Juvenile Books, 1995. Book and cassette.

Videos

Jewels of the Caribbean Sea, National Geographic, 1995.

Ocean Drifters, National Geographic, 1995.

Web Sites

Adopt a Turtle, the Caribbean Conservation Corporation Founded by Archie Carr, it's dedicated to sea turtle conservation. Adopted sea turtles are tracked via satellite. For more information: www.cccturtle.org.

Encyclopedia Mythica
Check out more myths and legends at www.pantheon.org/mythica.html.

Chapter 3: Explore Sea Gardens and Tide Pools

Videos

Australia's Great Barrier Reef, National Geographic, 1993.

Treasures of the Great Barrier Reef, NOVA, 1995.

Chapter 4: Search Out Ocean Meadows and Mermaids

Videos

The Little Mermaid, Disney, 1989.

Thirteenth Year, Buena Vista Home Video, 1999.

Web Sites

Project Seahorse
You can support Project Seahorse's efforts by shopping at the Shedd Aquarium's Big Blue shop, which displays products crafted in Handumon. Big Blue has partnered with Project Seahorse by selling straw hats, totes, beach mats,

rattan pencil cases, sunglasses holders, and lanka-wood model boats handcrafted from environmentally safe materials. A hangtag on each item tells about the Project Seahorse mission in Handumon. Money from the sales of these products supports sea horse conservation. Information on Project Seahorse: www.seahorse.mcgill.ca.

Ollie Otter Lunch Bag Puppet and Kelp Forest coloring page from the Monterey Bay Aquarium
www.mbayaq.org/lc/kids_place/kidseq_pnd_otter.asp

Sea Otter Cam at the Monterey Bay Aquarium
www.mbayaq.org/efc/efc_fo/fo_ottr_cam.asp

See sea horse short movies at Seahorse World.
www.seahorseworld.com.au

Chapter 5: Dive into the Deep

Books

Osborne, Mary Pope. *Mermaid Tales from Around the World*. New York: Scholastic Trade, 1999.

Yolen, Jane, and Shulamith Oppenheim. *The Fish Prince and Other Stories, Mermen Folk Tales*. Northampton, MA: Interlink Publishing Group, Inc., 2001.

Web Sites

Check out real ocean research with the scientists at Dive and Discover: Expeditions to the Seafloor. You'll find daily updates on their research and findings as they explore the deep ocean.
www.divediscover.whoi.edu

Take a look at the wonderful photos of the mimic octopus. You'll be amazed at this octopus magician.
www.asian-diver.com/themagazine/marinelife/mimicoct.html

Chapter 6: Gone Fishing

Web Sites

Learn more about the art of gyotaku and see a gallery of completed work.
www.hawaiianfishprints.com

Take a look at some Mexican yarn paintings at Huichol Art Online.
www.huicholartonline.com

Learn more about marine fish conservation at the National Coalition for Marine Conservation Web site.
www.savethefish.org

Chapter 7: Search for Shells, Sand, and Surprises

Books

Lindbergh, Anne Morrow. *Gift from the Sea*. New York: Pantheon Press, 1991.

Williams, Winston. *Florida's Fabulous Seashells and Seashore Life*. Tampa, FL: World Publications, 1988.

Web Sites

Check out artist Sandy Maron's sailor's valentines at www.sailorsvalentinestudio.com.

Visit the Beaches section of the National Park System Web site to find out information on individual parks. www.nps.gov

➡ *California*

Point Reyes
Point Reyes National Seashore
Dunes, bluffs, lagoons, tall cliffs, and long, broad beaches north of San Francisco.

San Diego
Cabrillo National Monument
It has tide pools, whale watching, and a lighthouse.

Santa Barbara
Channel Islands National Monument
Anacapa, seals, sea lions, and sea elephants.

➡ *Florida*

Fort Jefferson, Key West
Dry Tortugas National Park
Seven small coral islands and terns.

Near Miami, Naples, and Homestead
Everglades National Park
Subtropical wilderness, small islands in Gulf of Mexico and Florida Bay, waterfowl, alligators, and loggerhead turtles.

➡ *Maine*

Near Bar Harbor
Acadia National Park
Mount Desert Island, tide pools, cliffs, sea birds, and scenic rocky coast.

➡ *Maryland*

Berlin
Assateague Island National Seashore

➡ *Massachusetts*

Wellfleet
Cape Cod National Seashore
Broad beaches, dunes, cliffs, marshes, and seaside villages.

➡ *New York*

Fire Island
Fire Island National Seashore
Barrier island off Long Island, firm beaches, dunes, and salt marshes.

➡ *North Carolina*

Cape Hatteras
Cape Hatteras National Seashore
Chain of barrier islands that extends for 70 miles (112.7 kilometers), broad beaches, dunes, and seaside villages.

Cape Hatteras
Pea Island National Wildlife Refuge
Dolphin sightings.

➤ *Texas*

Padre Island
Padre Island National Seashore
Eighty miles (128.8 kilometers) of barrier island seashore, shells, birds, and broad, sandy beaches.

➤ *Virgin Islands, Caribbean*

Virgin Islands National Park
Tropical island park featuring coral reefs, sandy beaches, tropical vegetation, and underwater nature trails.

➤ *Virginia*

Chincoteague
Chincoteague National Wildlife Refuge
Wild ponies, marshes, waterfowl, and sandy beaches.

➤ *Washington*

Port Angeles
Olympic National Park
Fifty miles (80.5 kilometers) of Pacific coastline, sandy beaches, rocky cliffs, tide pools, and seals.

Chapter 8: Beware Sharks!

Books

Martin, Rafe. *The Shark God*. New York: Scholastic, 2001.

McGovern, Ann. *Shark Lady: True Adventures of Eugenie Clark*. New York: Scholastic, 1978.

Web Sites

Wild Aid
Check out this organization's Web site for up-to-date information on its shark campaign and Peter Benchley's involvement. You will find out more about the practice of shark finning and other threats to shark populations. www.wildaid.org

Chapter 9: Have a Whale of a Time

Music

Paul Winter Consort. *Songs of the Humpback Whale and Whales Alive*.

Raffi. *Baby Beluga*. (There is also a book by the same title.)

Videos

Dolphins, look for it at an IMAX theater, narrated by Pierce Brosnan and featuring Sting, 2000.

Dolphins: The Wild Side, National Geographic, 1999.

Flipper, Universal Studios, 1998.

Free Willy, Warner Studios, 1993.

The Free Willy Story: Keiko's Journey Home, Discovery Home Video, 1998.

In the Wild: Dolphins with Robin Williams, PBS Home Video, 1997.

Star Trek IV: The Voyage Home, Paramount, 1986.

Web Sites

Print out whale and dolphin coloring book pages.
www.enchantedlearning.com/crafts/books/whalebook

Find out how marine mammals are trained.
www.seaworld.org/animal_training/mmtrain

Check out real killer whales at Sea World on Shamu Cam.
www.shamu.com/html/shamuCam.html

Chapter 10: Travel Icy Seas and Glaciers

Books

Berger, Melvin. *Oil Spill! (Let's Read and Find Out)*. New York:
Harper Trophy, 1994.

Web Sites

Penguin Cam at the Monterey Aquarium
http://www.mbayaq.org/efc/efc_fo/fo_peng_camlive.asp

The Penguin Page
http://home.capu.net/~kwelch/penguins/

More Ocean Organizations

American Oceans Campaign
(323) 936-8242, www.americanocean.org

Center for Marine Conservation
 www.cmc-ocean.org

Coast Alliance
(202) 546-9554, www.coastalliance.org

Cousteau Society
(800) 441-4395, www.cousteausociety.org

Greenpeace
(800) 326-0959, www.greenpeace.org

National Audubon Society
www.audubon.org

Wildlife Conservation Society
(718) 220-5100, www.wcs.org

Ocean Challenges

Chapter 1
How many seas can you find on a world map or globe?
Which ones are true seas?

Chapter 2
Take a bucketful of water from the sunlit layer of the ocean.
Take a look into the bucket. What do you see? If it looks
clear to you look again, but this time take a small amount
out and look at it under a microscope. Now what do you
see? Share your findings with a friend.

Chapter 3
Many coral species are named for the way they look. There
is bubble coral, tree coral, and brain coral. There is even
lettuce coral. Try drawing what you think brain coral might
look like.

Chapter 4
Find out about other Japanese foods that incorporate
seaweed. Find a restaurant in your area where you can
sample some of these dishes.

Chapter 5
Who invented the periscope? Where is the periscope most
often used?

Chapter 6
➤ Which of the following are true fish?

Octopus	*Crab*
Skate	*Tuna*
Barracuda	*Mudskipper*
Eel	*Herring*
Shark	

Just as you can look at the rings on a tree trunk to measure the age of the tree, you can look at the rings on the scales of a fish to measure the age of the fish. Take a look at the fish you caught. Ask the grown-up to remove a few scales for you from below the lateral line of the fish. Examine the scales under a microscope. You will see rings on the scales. Some will be close together and some will be farther apart. The closer the rings, the slower the fish was growing, and the farther apart the rings, the faster the fish was growing. Usually, fish growth slows during the winter months. Can you tell how old the fish is?

fish scales

scale showing growth rings

Chapter 7

Take a few moments and think of all the different places you've seen shell designs. I bet you'll think of a lot! Maybe you've seen a shell design in a piece of molding in your home or printed on wallpaper. Where else have you seen shell designs in your home? Think about designs of jewelry, fabric, and picture frames. Take the shell scavenger hunt challenge and see how many shell designs you can find in your home. Did you find many different shell shapes or mostly the scallop shell shape?

Chapter 8

Compare a shark tooth with a human tooth. Look at other animal teeth. Can you tell what kinds of food they eat by looking at their teeth?

Chapter 9

Try making some other origami animals. Can you make a dolphin?

Chapter 10

Go clam digging with a grown-up. Follow local regulations for digging. You'll need a bucket and a shovel. Wear boots or old sneakers that you don't mind getting wet. Look for holes in the sand that indicate a clam is below—usually the bigger the hole, the bigger the clam. Start digging about six inches away on either side of the hole. You will probably have to dig down about a foot or more to find your clam. Have a grown-up help you. When you find the clam, rinse it off with water to remove the sand or mud. Examine the clam's shell and note its pattern. When you're through you can either take it home to eat it or place it back where you found it.

Index

Also Available

Winter Day Play!

Activities, Crafts, and Games for Indoors and Out
Nancy F. Castaldo

A Smithsonian Notable Book for Children

"Playful and informative text."
  —*KIDS Magazine*

"Help children learn, explore, and have fun all winter long. Ideal
  for one child or the entire classroom."
  —*Arts & Activities*

Snow painting with spray bottles filled with food coloring, making
snow cream with fresh fallen snow, or building Japanese snow
cottages are a few of the more than 70 activities that will keep kids
busy learning, exploring, and having fun all winter long.

Ages 3 and up
176 pages, 10 x 8
Illustrated throughout
Paperback, $13.95
ISBN 1-55652-381-5

How the Earth Works

**60 Fun Activities for Exploring Volcanoes, Fossils, Earthquakes,
  and More**
Michelle O'Brien-Palmer

A Selection of the Teacher Book Club

Earth science erupts with 60 hands-on activities such as "core
sampling" a filled cupcake; learning about plate tectonics by floating
graham crackers on a molten mantle of molasses; fossilizing plastic
insects; and, of course, the classic volcano demonstrations. Several
of the activities involve food, and teaching your way through snack
time is a great way to sneak in some science.

Ages 6–9
194 pages, 9¼ x 7
Illustrated throughout
Paperback, $14.95
ISBN 1-55652-442-0

Both books are available at your local bookstore, or call 1-800-888-4741.

CHICAGO
REVIEW
PRESS

Distributed by Independent Publishers Group
www.ipgbook.com